NOT A GENTLEMAN'S WORK

NOT A GENTLEMAN'S WORK

THE UNTOLD STORY OF
A GRUESOME MURDER AT SEA AND
THE LONG ROAD TO TRUTH

GERARD KOEPPEL

hachette
BOOKS
NEW YORK

Hachette Books
Hachette Book Group
1290 Avenue of the Americas
New York, NY 10104
HachetteBooks.com
Twitter.com/HachetteBooks
Instagram.com/HachetteBooks

First Edition: June 2020

Hachette Books is a division of Hachette Book Group, Inc.

The Hachette Books name and logo are trademarks of Hachette Book Group, Inc.

The publisher is not responsible for websites (or their content) that are not owned by the publisher.

Print book interior design by Trish Wilkinson

Library of Congress Cataloging-in-Publication Data

Names: Koeppel, Gerard T., 1957– author.
Title: Not a gentleman's work: the untold story of a gruesome murder at sea and the long road to truth / Gerard Koeppel.
Identifiers: LCCN 2019056404 | ISBN 9780306903380 (hardcover) | ISBN 9780306903403 (ebook)
Subjects: LCSH: Herbert Fuller (Ship) | Monks, Lester Hawthorne, 1876- | Bram, Thomas. | Murder—Atlantic Ocean—Case studies. | Murder—Investigation—Nova Scotia—Halifax—Case studies.
Classification: LCC HV6535.A78 K64 2020 | DDC 364.152/3092 [B]—dc23
LC record available at https://lccn.loc.gov/2019056404

ISBNs: 978-0-306-90338-0 (hardcover), 978-0-306-90340-3 (e-book), 978-1-5491-0187-8 (audio)

Printed in the United States of America

LSC-C

10 9 8 7 6 5 4 3 2 1

For Diane, Jackson, Harry, Kate, and Scrappy

CONTENTS

"You're a gentleman," they used to say. "You shouldn't hack about with an axe; that's not a gentleman's work."

—DOSTOEVSKY, *CRIME AND PUNISHMENT* (1867)

PROLOGUE

A MAN WITH MEANS

Men hold boats in the secret place of their mind, almost
from the cradle to the grave.

—E. B. White,
"The Sea and the Wind That Blows" (1963)

"I am thinking of going travelling for a year, and I expect to
take a passage in this vessel to South America; what do you
think of it?"

The question was put by Lester Monks, age twenty, of Boston,
to Thomas Bram, thirty-two, newly signed first mate of the *Herbert Fuller*, the sailing ship on which Monks expected to take passage. This was the afternoon of June 16, 1896. The *Fuller* was tied
up along Mystic Wharf in Boston's harbor, loading in her holds
and on deck a cargo of New England pine boards. The lumber was
destined for Rosario, up the Parana River from Buenos Aires, six
thousand ocean miles from Boston. The long voyage to Argentina
was scheduled to begin early the following month. As first mate,
hired six days earlier, Bram was overseeing the preparations.

"Well, if I was a man with means," said Bram, eying the young
gentleman, "and intended to travel for a year, I would go in a
steamer, because you would get better accommodations, it would

1

be more pleasant, and you will have a great deal more to see and learn than you would on board a small vessel."

In 1896, Octave Chanute designed the glider that the Wright brothers famously adapted, Henry Flagler extended his Florida railroad to the settlement that would become Miami, the staged crash of two speeding locomotives in rural Texas drew forty thousand people and killed three of them, and Henry Ford built his first car. The *Herbert Fuller* also became famous that summer, quite unexpectedly, as it was an unremarkable ship.

The *Fuller* was built in Maine during 1890; the November launching was reported, briefly, in Boston and New York newspapers. The ship was named for one of its owners, a founder and vice president of the ship's underwriter, Boston Marine Insurance Company, which was among the country's largest insurers. The ship's ownership was divided into 128 shares. The land-based Herbert Fuller owned 4 shares, which for some reason came with naming honors that he came to regret. The ship's lasting infamy would substantially eclipse its namesake's good business reputation.

The *Fuller*, a sturdy barkentine, was 175 feet from stem to stern—not the greatest vessel, but one adequately sized for the intended voyage. The ship had sailed the route and many others without serious incident for six years under builder, principal owner, and captain Charles Nash.

"And another thing," said Bram, "we will be about 60 or 70 days on the passage." Bram assumed that Monks was an entire stranger, a young man of means visiting the waterfront for his amusement or distraction, engaging in idle small talk with men who were otherwise busy with work.

In fact, Monks replied, he wanted "a sea voyage for my health because it would take so much longer." Thus, a sailing ship was preferred: "I intend to go anyway in this vessel."

Monks made it seem that his voyaging was a matter of personal choice. It was not. This was the first time Monks had met

Bram, but it was Monks's third visit to the *Herbert Fuller* in recent days, the prior visits having been with his father. Lester first met Nash in a shipping agent's office. "I wanted to look the captain over," Lester later said, "and see if I thought I would like him before I engaged passage." Lester's preferences didn't matter. His father had arranged his son's meeting and his passage. Monks was going with Nash whether he liked the captain or not.

The senior Monks had already made careful inquiries about the ship and its master. He was told by a shipping agency he could "rest easy," as the ship "was safe, weatherly, and manned by a captain who knew his business and attended to it." Frank Monks felt comfortable that Nash "was a very reliable man," had respectable connections in Maine, was in every way a capable navigator, and "I could entrust my son to his care."

Bram didn't know that Lester was dissembling about his agency in his upcoming voyage. As Monks later acknowledged in a sworn statement, he took passage on the *Herbert Fuller* "under the advice and at the request of my parents."

Lester's intentions were not relevant. Frank Monks's intention was that his son get as far away from Boston for as long as possible. A few months as a passenger on a sailing ship to Argentina was just the start. The expectation was that a voyage from South America to Europe would follow. A return to Boston might be arranged at some point, but there was no hurry.

Why did Frank Monks, respected Boston businessman, want his elder son gone? He committed no crime or dishonor. He had only, it seems, gotten himself thrown out of Harvard, for having done little work and much drinking. There was one element of truth in what Lester Monks told Thomas Bram: the sea voyage was for Monks's health, in that the long voyage was intended to sever his consumption of alcohol.

Unfortunately, Frank Monks did not inspect his son's extensive luggage, which included sixty bottles of beer and a quart each of whiskey and brandy: not fuel for a ten-week debauch but enough to ease withdrawal and arouse trouble, to which Lester was prone. His drinking supplies would be kept in the ship's storeroom, directly across the main cabin from Lester's sleeping quarters. Aside from ship supplies and Monks's liquor, the storeroom featured an important emergency item, hung in brass fittings on the aft wall: a shiny new axe.

A sailing ship's axe is rarely used, its primary purpose being to cut away rigging when a mast that could puncture the hull comes down in a storm. The axe is practically never used to kill people.

1

THE PASSENGER

He . . . never had any infantile troubles.
—Frank Monks on son Lester,
"Monks Memorabilia"

The first son of Frank and Elizabeth Monks was born as a blank. The birth registry of Brookline, Massachusetts, for April 27, 1876, says Frank Hawthorne Monks, merchant, and Elizabeth Crowell Monks, wife, themselves both born in nearby Boston, had a son born at their home on Monmouth Street with no given name. Maybe the birth was registered before the parents could agree on or commit to a name. Perhaps it was just an accident of timing: the name had been chosen but not communicated to the registrar. In any case, it was a small irregularity at the outset of a life that would grow substantially more irregular.

Soon enough, the son was given the name Lester Hawthorne. The middle name of father and son was not, as it might suggest, homage to the famous author, born and buried in Salem, a short distance up the coast from Boston. The Monkses were not a literary family. No, the middle name was given merely for Nancy Hawthorne, Frank's mother's paternal grandmother, of Hampton, Virginia. Nancy was widowed when her husband, William

Hatton, was knocked overboard by a sailboat boom and drowned; she died soon after, resurrected nominally among the Monkses.

Lester, meanwhile, was a name original in the family lines, intended perhaps to suggest some Anglo lineage—the name derives from the ancient English city Leicester—to a boy whose paternal grandfather had arrived poor from Ireland. Lester's older sister was Marion, and his younger brother would be Archibald, both old Anglo names, like Lester new to the family.

Initially, Lester created a favorable impression. "He was one of the handsomest babies I ever saw," thought his father. "He was very strong and robust and never had any infantile troubles." Frank Monks wrote this in 1894, at the threshold of Lester's early adult troubles.

Lester Monks's story "is a potential epic that someone should have researched thoroughly and written up." This was the opinion in 1978 of his much younger cousin the Reverend G. Gardner Monks, in his memoirs privately published and distributed to a score of family members on his eightieth birthday. "Long before I ever met him, from many family conversations I got the clear impression that he was a skeleton in the family closet who must at all times be kept carefully out of sight."

The reverend was utterly respectable: Harvard, Oxford, Union Theological in New York, Episcopal Theological in his native Boston, where the Monkses in America began in 1830. Reverend Monks was the first headmaster of the storied Lenox School for two decades, then canon of Washington Cathedral for ten years and afterward St. Paul's in Boston for seven years, before commencing an active retirement in Maine in 1965. Many decades earlier, Lester had proved entirely unrespectable, yet for the young reverend it "is well to admit . . . that he was my favorite cousin." Reverend Monks had a number of cousins to choose from, but Lester, dead before the reverend turned thirty, was a lifelong fascination.

WHEN OLIVER WENDELL Holmes decreed certain families the Brahmin caste of New England in 1860, the Boston Monkses were not in the running. Though several of them achieved highly, the family could never reach the heights of Boston society.

The first American Monks, John Patrick, was born poor and Catholic near Dublin in 1804. Little is known of his parents, other than that at some point his father kept a roadside inn. Otherwise, the Monkses in Ireland are "a near total void of information." That is, hardly Brahmin provenance.

At seventeen, John was apprenticed to a shipwright in Liverpool; four years later, he was in Nova Scotia working as a shipwright himself, with a small lumber business on the side. Seeking broader opportunity, John Monks moved on to Boston in 1830 and worked for a shipbuilder. In 1832, he married Catherine Mary Erskine, a nineteen-year-old from Ireland. Around the time of his marriage, John brought a large cargo of timber from Maine and turned it into deck planking for ships. In time, he was a major lumber merchant.

John and Catherine had three children who would live into adulthood—William, born in 1833, Catherine in 1834, and Richard in 1836—followed by two daughters who died in infancy. After five pregnancies before age thirty, Catherine Monks gave out in 1843.

Just over a year after Catherine's death, John Monks married Delia Smith Hatton, born in 1818, from a Baptist family tracing substantial American roots back to the mid-1600s; she was the granddaughter of Nancy Hawthorne Hatton. Here was some proper American heritage for the Monkses to attach to. John and Delia had five children: Henry Grafton, born in 1846; Louisa in 1848; Frank Hawthorne, father of Lester, in 1850; George Howard in 1853; and Robert Hatton in 1856. "We were a very united family with few disagreements," George recalled many years later, "and our family life was a very happy one." Any disagreement with his assessment is not recorded.

By the early 1850s, John Monks was thriving. He was listed among fifteen hundred "Rich Men of Massachusetts" in 1851, with a worth of $200,000: "Began poor. Born in Ireland. An extensive dealer in, and sawer of ship-timber," reads his entry, brief, like most. Nearly half of those listed had begun poor like Monks. His worth put him firmly above the average rich man; only three hundred or so were worth more. He was worth more—in dollars, that is—than, for example, Harvard-educated lawyer Sidney Bartlett ($150,000), whose Harvard-educated son Francis would become the Monks family attorney.

During the 1850s, Monks added real estate investment to his lumber wealth. Among his purchases was a commercial building in Congress Square that would become the locus of family business in succeeding generations. The original Monks Building at 35 Congress Street was destroyed in the great Boston fire of 1872 and replaced by the family with a handsome new building there, designed by prominent Massachusetts architect Alexander Rice Esty. The building survives; the Monks name remained over the main entrance into the 1960s.

In the meantime, fatal illness intervened. John's oldest son, William, was sent to Europe in 1858 in hopes of curing a lung disease; he died in France the following May, with his father and stepmother at his bedside. They returned to Boston in July. In December, John Monks died of the same disease, leaving Delia with seven young children but enough money to live well. By 1864, the family was at 61 Chester Square, "a very comfortable and cheerful house" at a fashionable address (as 556 Massachusetts Avenue, less so today).

John's daughter Catherine improved the Monkses' connections in 1863 by marrying Horace Standish Bradford, of two Brahmin families. Catherine's half brother George would enter the family in a fully Brahmin line by marrying Olga Eliza Gardner in June 1897. Boston society would be well represented in the wedding party and on the guest list, which included longtime US Supreme Court associate justice Horace Gray.

The Monks family forged associations with Harvard via three of John and Delia's four sons. Henry graduated in 1867 and George from the college in 1875 and the medical school in 1880. Robert, artistically inclined like his mother, did not go to Harvard (or any other college) but married fellow artist Anne Bellows Hill, a daughter of the Reverend Thomas Hill, a Harvard graduate (A.B. 1843, D. Div. 1845) and Harvard president during the 1860s. Robert and Anne married in 1881; five years later, her older sister Elizabeth married Dr. Alfred Worcester, a three-degree Harvard man. Worcester became a renowned pioneer in various aspects of medical care and, in 1950, the oldest living Harvard graduate. A half century earlier, he became the physician in close charge of his sister-in-law's alcoholic nephew, Lester Monks.

Of John and Delia's four sons, only Lester's father, Frank, had no Harvard connection. After proper preparatory schools—Boston Latin and the Greylock Institute —he eschewed college for a business partnership with his considerably older half brother Richard. In 1868, they formed Monks and Company, flour and grain merchants in Boston. Nine months later, a serious illness forced Richard to retire from business for a period, and the partnership folded. Frank, just nineteen years old, stayed in the flour business, soon partnering with an older sales agent who moved to Boston from Ohio. The partnership, Smith & Monks, flourished. Meanwhile, Frank married Elizabeth "Lisbeth" Oakford Crowell, of an old Maine family who had established themselves in Boston; the Crowell home at 51 Chester Square made them close neighbors of the Monkses. Frank and Elizabeth had known each other as neighborhood children, and "hence there was no occasion for a long courtship." Engaged on Christmas Day 1871, they married the following October, at her parents' house. He was twenty-one, she nineteen.

By then, half brother Richard had recovered, and, while remaining in the flour business with Kyse Smith, Frank partnered again with Richard, forming Monks Brothers, this time in banking and brokerage. Both of Frank's businesses had offices in the Monks Building. The business with Richard soon failed again, but the flour business with Smith boomed.

When Elizabeth was pregnant with Lester, the family moved out to Brookline and then, after Archie was born in 1879, to a larger Brookline house. In 1889, with his partner readying to retire and presciently sensing a downturn in the Boston-based flour business, Frank switched to local railroads; among other positions, he became general manager of the West End Street Railroad Company, whose cars ran through a substantial portion of Boston streets. Frank also became a trustee with Richard of their father's substantial estate. Frank, wrote his younger brother George, "was industrious and able, and was a devoted son to my mother and a good brother to me."

Frank was also a good father, particularly supportive of Lester's early interest in boats. At a young age, Lester became "passionately fond of yachting," facilitated during family summers at various rented houses on the Massachusetts coast. At twelve, Lester proved himself seamanlike beyond his years. He was on a boat sailed by older and supposedly wiser sailors who lost control in a squall. Lester watched as the sails tore and the boat took on water. He then suggested that the boat's tender, towed astern, be filled with water to use as a drag and keep the sailboat's bow into the sea instead of dangerously broadside to it. This was done, "and the squall was ridden out in safety."

Two summers later came a more harrowing experience. Lester and his good friend Guy Hamilton Scull, a future Harvard classmate and later brave and famous world adventurer, set off with two other boys on a sailing trip from Marblehead around Cape Ann to York Harbor on the southern Maine coast and back, a voyage of some ninety mostly open-water miles. Lester and Guy manned Guy's twenty-foot centerboard catboat, the other two boys in a less comfortable but faster and more seaworthy twenty-one-foot sloop. The boys were fourteen; it was their first long cruise. The boats had cabins barely large enough for sleep and a small amount of eatable provisions. "There was," wrote one boy, "the complete freedom of life, and the excitement of relying on our own skill and judgment for the first time." Parents who let boys of this age make such a voyage today would be prosecuted, or at least abused on Twitter.

The boys sailed north without incident. On the return the following day, the thirty miles from York Harbor across Ipswich Bay to the turning point at Cape Ann turned rough late in the afternoon. The boats sailed toward a "very black looking squall" a few miles from the cape. The boys on the quicker boat looked anxiously at the other boat, which was nearly a mile to leeward, "and wonder[ed] whether they would be all right." As it happened, the squall had no violent winds, and the quicker boat got past the cape with ease and found a mooring in Gloucester Harbor at ten at night.

The other boat, meanwhile, had much harder going. While reefing, they were blown off course and seaward. Then the wind dropped, and they had a long, slow nighttime beat toward Gloucester. For a while, they noticed a red light that they thought far ahead. Then the light was upon them: the port running light of a coasting schooner that nearly ran down the boys' small unlit boat.

They finally made their way into Gloucester at five in the morning and tied up to the stern of their cruising companion, all cheer: "There was Lester Monks . . . grinning down the hatch at us." He and Guy had sailed the whole night without sleep or worry. Six summers later, Lester would claim to be a habitual heavy sleeper who had slumbered through three axe murders occurring within a few feet of him.

At sixteen, Lester was "the youngest helmsman on the coast" around Marblehead, where his racing prowess became well known.

For the summer of 1895, he purchased *Bessie*, a "fast and able" twenty-six-foot Cape catboat, in "perfect condition," with a large inventory of sails and equipment. "As an amateur skipper there are few better in the bay than Lester Monks," said his Marblehead friends. On the breeze-filled final weekend of July, he put his boat to the test. "Lester Monks was trying to see how far down he could put his sloop Bessie without taking [on] water; she took many strong puffs, and proved herself a very able boat." Whether such a test proved Lester a very able skipper is less clear.

Summers were Lester's distinguished season. The other seasons involved school. He attended Noble & Greenough and Boston Latin, both feeders for Harvard. His scholastic record is unavailable, but it presumably was with good reason that Lester applied not to Harvard per se but to the Lawrence Scientific School, then an independent undergraduate geology program at Harvard with considerably less rigid acceptance standards. On his admission exam for Lawrence Scientific, Lester scored Cs in Chemistry, Algebra, and History. That was the high ground. In Physics, Plane and Solid Geometry, English, and French, it was all Ds. Perhaps other students were admitted with worse, but the family name apparently was good enough for Lester to matriculate in the fall of 1894.

During its six-decade run, ending in 1906 when it was incorporated into Harvard generally (its institutional descendant is the Harvard John A. Paulson School of Engineering and Applied Sciences), Lawrence Scientific had many distinguished students. The roll notably includes zoologist Alexander Agassiz, Louis's equally accomplished son; botanist Daniel Cady Eaton, grandson of pioneering botanist Amos; botanist Horace Mann Jr., son of the educator; Harvard Medical School dean Henry Bowditch, grandson of mathematician and maritime navigation pioneer Nathaniel; hydraulic engineer Clemens Herschel; Union army general and Medal of Honor recipient Horace Porter; board-game pioneer Milton

Bradley; philosopher William James; New York philanthropist Philip Schuyler; and 1896 Olympic triple-jump champion James Brendan Connolly, who had to quit college in order to compete.

Lester Monks, as his entry exams might have foretold, did not become one of this illustrious company. Freshman year he excelled in Geology, relative, that is, to his other courses: a D, over failing Es in English, German, Chemistry 2, and Physics. His second year, which was not as a sophomore but as a repeat freshman, started better but rapidly tailed. In November, a C in Chemistry 1, a C– in German, a D in Physics 1, and an E in English. The mid-year grades fell to two Es and two Ds, plus an E in Chemistry 2 (apparently a second attempt after the prior year's E). By April, Lester was down to three Es and a D, and Chemistry 2 was missing. No final grades were reported.

Lester's grades were bad at least in part because his absences were many. On November 8, 1894, during his first semester, he was unable to attend lectures "on account of sickness," the ailment unspecified in his required explanatory note to Montague Chamberlain, the school secretary (and ornithologist of some note). A form filed upon his return to classes the next day indicated the absence was due to "bad cold and jams in bowels," an interesting combination. "His father fears pneumonia, which the boy has suffered from twice," Chamberlain wrote on the form. On December 14, what Monks called tonsillitis occasioned another absence. The next day, the school dean, Nathaniel Shaler (who remains a revered career Harvardian despite his overt racism and Anglo supremacism), wrote the senior Monks that Lester "is not doing as well as he ought to do in his work."

"I hear this with the greatest regret," Mr. Monks replied to Chamberlain, "and assure you that I will do all in my power to bring about a change in this matter. . . . I feel confident that I shall be able to work very much more effectively . . . if I am kept advised of the condition of affairs respecting my son's work."

If there was regular communication and monitoring, it is not recorded. Lester's grades and attendance deteriorated.

The following fall, he was absent "a great deal." In December 1895, Lester's uncle and Harvard professor George informed Chamberlain that "Lester seems now to be all right again. He is up and about" and anticipating a return to classes in the new year. "I shall take especial pains to urge upon him the necessity for work in order that his enforced absence from college may not count against him too much at the end of the year."

Again, the situation did not improve. In late January 1896, Lester wrote a long note to Shaler, seeking to explain his absence for much of the month, again "having been sick a great deal" and promising improved performance on his spring midyears. Unfortunately, "cold and headaches, continuation of old troubles," kept him out of school for twelve days in February. In April came a new ailment: "in bed with bad knee and fever results of a bicycle accident." The knee makes sense; the fever casts doubt. But the incident does call to mind an alarming tendency that had been noted recently by the *New York Times*: "There is not the slightest doubt that bicycle riding, if persisted in, leads to weakness of mind, general lunacy, and homicidal mania." In any case, Lester's ailments prevented class attendance from April 18 to May 5. He presumably also missed classes on April 14, when he served as usher for the Tuesday midday wedding of his sister, Marion.

Lester Monks's college days were effectively over. "I have decided that it is best for me to leave the Scientific School," he wrote to Chamberlain at the end of May 1896, as if there was any doubt of his status. "My health has been so poor for the last two years, with no prospect of a change for the better, that it seems [best not] to continue my course." Before his signature, Lester managed, "Thanking you for your kindness and interest toward me." A handwritten notation in blue ink at the top of the page—"agreed," over Shaler's signature—is the final word on Lester Monks's brief and troubled Harvard career. Five weeks later, he was aboard the *Herbert Fuller*.

What ruined Lester at Harvard was neither physical ailment nor insufficient intelligence but liquor. "Doubtless alcohol," wrote his cousin, "was a major problem even this early. Many of his escapades were apparently a good deal less than innocent." Lester's oversight of a sleigh notoriously hoisted to the roof of a Harvard dorm was generally understood to have been alcohol fueled.

It would be said later, in courts, newspapers, and books, that Lester Monks left Harvard after his second year on account of bronchial or related health issues. To be sure, he had them, but they derived from one particular health issue: "alcohol, which was to prove the curse of his adult life."

Precisely when, how, and why Lester's life became alcohol infused is impossible to know. In the generations of American Monks, there are no apparent alcohol issues. Alcoholism did not run in Lester's bloodlines. Undoubtedly, something troubled Lester, before his arrival at Harvard. What it was perhaps was unknown even to him. But it shaped his behavior and affected his fate.

Though a number of Monks passed through Harvard successfully before and after Lester, it was never the place for him. With Lester's removal from Harvard, his family decided a long sea voyage might cure him or at least keep him far away to avoid further family embarrassment. The decision was made quickly. Two days after his letter formally withdrawing from the Lawrence Scientific School, Lester placed a "For Sale" notice in the *Boston Herald* for his catboat, *Bessie*; they would not be racing that summer. Inquiries were made by his parents for a suitable ship for a long voyage, and the *Herbert Fuller* was selected.

We know that Lester brought with him a supply of alcohol. He also brought something that can go very poorly with alcohol—a gun. "Just before I started on what I thought was to be such an enjoyable and health-giving trip, I happened to think of the desirability of getting a revolver. At first I had decided not to get one, but happening to be near a gun store in Boston, and having some spare change, I went in and purchased the firearm." As he later told reporters in Halifax, "That fact unquestionably explains why I am here today a live man."

It is certainly true that Lester's revolver would help him get back to shore alive. The trouble with his whimsical tale is that it is a lie. In fact, as he would eventually testify under oath, the revolver "was given to me by my uncle." Uncle George, the father of Lester's later charmed younger cousin Gardner, was among the relatives who came to see Lester off. He told Lester that "he still believed in him," that he "had a chance and a good one" to get over his troubles, "but it was now or never." The older man also noted a lumber ship was not a yacht and its voyage no cruise. "So, I have brought you this": a revolver plus a box of cartridges.

Lester Monks would never be asked to explain why he lied about how he came to be armed. It is understandable perhaps that the prosecutors didn't ask—it might have deflected from their case against the accused—but it is inexplicable that the generally heroic defense attorneys, needing to shift blame elsewhere, would never seek to catch Lester in this lie.

2

THE MATE

Thomas was always a good boy [and] good boys make good men.

—Caroline Bram, mother of Thomas,
Boston Globe, April 7, 1897

Thomas Bram had had a full life on land and sea before fate put him aboard the *Herbert Fuller* at age thirty-two.

Bram was born in February 1864 on St. Kitts, one of the Windward Islands in the Caribbean. The day varies from document to document, but his death certificate says February 3, so that will be the last word. His full name was Thomas Mead Chambers Bram. His parents appear to have been—the record is thin—Daniel Burnet Bram, a native of Dutch Guiana who arrived at St. Kitts as a ship's cook and settled there as a shoemaker, and Caroline T. Gibbs, a St. Kitts native. Somewhat incredibly, his lawyer would later say his mother "was an English woman and his father a Dutchman," which was true only in the very broadest of senses. Despite Thomas Bram's lifelong assertion of whiteness, both his parents were of substantially African descent, though they each may have had whites in their lineage. They had three children: Thomas first, then Christina Elizabeth in 1865, and Levi Albert

Gibbs in 1867. While the children were young, Daniel Bram left his family in St. Kitts for places and a fate unknown.

The fate of Bram's younger brother, Levi, is also unknown; there are reports he was aboard a US-bound ship that sank with all aboard, ship and date unspecified. Bram's sister, Christina, stayed in St. Kitts, married, and had three children. Bram's mother and sister were "very intelligent and respectable people," and the family had "an excellent reputation all over the island." As for Bram himself, "He was as good a boy as ever lived here," said a relative, "and as bright as a dollar." "Thomas was always a good boy," said his mother, and "good boys make good men." She said this in early 1897, though she hadn't spoken to her elder son in many years.

Bram left St. Kitts at age sixteen, in 1879. "I ran away from home—that is, I shipped on a little schooner . . . unbeknownst to my mother." He never saw her or any family member again. The schooner brought him to New York; from there, he shipped as an ordinary seaman on another small schooner in the sardine trade between Maine and New York. After a year, he came ashore, soon finding employment in Manhattan as a waiter at a Dennett's restaurant, then a flourishing regional chain of religious-themed eateries that Alfred W. Dennett had started in 1876 in downtown Manhattan.

The religious aspects of the Dennett's restaurants, which featured inspirational quotations on the walls and prayer meetings, with cheap but decent food, apparently appealed to Bram, and Dennett took a liking to him. From waiter Bram was quickly promoted to assistant night manager, before being named manager of a Dennett's in Boston, at 239 Washington Street. Bram was popular there, "of such a genial disposition that he made many friends, not only among the employees of the place, but among the customers as well." In 1887, after a year in Boston, Bram returned to New York to be the manager of a large new Dennett's on Fourteenth Street at Fifth Avenue in Manhattan (now the site of New School University). After six months of getting that place established, Bram transferred to a Dennett's in Chicago. Three months later, it was back to New York to take charge of a small Dennett's on the Bowery.

The reason for the returns to New York was that Bram had gotten married, to a young woman he had met at his first Dennett's. Harriet—a.k.a. Hattie or Katie—Louise Hottenroth was two years younger than Bram. Her parents were German natives George Hottenroth and Louisa Hausser; they had each immigrated to New York as children with their respective families in the 1850s and married in 1864. Hattie was born in 1866, the first of an eventual eight children.

Just before he was named manager of the Boston Dennett's, Bram and Hattie had become engaged. He came back to New York after a week in Boston to marry her, on November 25, 1885, at the Franklin Street Methodist Episcopal Church in Manhattan, and they returned to Boston together, living for the year in a rented room in East Cambridge, before making a more permanent home back in Brooklyn near Hattie's parents. Her mother was not a fan: "Almost from the day of the marriage," she told a reporter seeking Bram insight in 1896, "he has scarcely done anything for Hattie's support."

He did make Hattie a mother, three times. Son William was born in 1887, Walter in 1889, and Herbert in 1892. After William's birth, the Dennett businesses failed; soon after opening restaurants ten years later in California, Dennett was struck and injured by a streetcar in San Francisco, lost his sanity, and died. In 1888, Bram bought the small restaurant he managed on the Bowery, but he couldn't make a go of it, sold it for a fraction of what he had paid, and went back to sea. He had been naturalized as an American citizen that year, enabling him to ship as an officer on American vessels. It meant extended periods away from home.

His mother-in-law may have welcomed or regretted Bram's departure. "He was a great talker but that was about all that he did," she said. According to her, besides his Bowery restaurant, Bram had opened a restaurant in Brooklyn "and was crooked in conducting that." His family knew nothing about it until, having run up bills "right and left" and paid nobody, Bram closed the restaurant, and creditors came after Hattie's father because Bram had used his father-in-law's name for credit. In any case, this was Mrs. Hottenroth's story.

Meanwhile, Bram was gone. Employed by G. A. Brett & Company, a New York brokerage that operated a number of ships, Bram served as first mate on a Maine schooner, then as captain and part owner of a small brig, the 160-ton *Twilight*, the purchase of which Bram himself negotiated for Brett in Maine. After that, there was one voyage as captain of a small schooner, *China*. "All our relations have been pleasant & satisfactory," the company attested in 1890. "He is a competent, honest & sober shipmaster."

Voyages in a variety of ships followed, with ports of call from Nova Scotia to the Gulf Coast, Cuba, and South America, shipping everything from kerosene and lumber to molasses and sugar on brigs and schooners. In 1892, Bram was living in New York again. Through his father-in-law, who knew an owner of the Manhattan Lighterage and Transportation Company, Bram became captain of a five-hundred-ton steam barge, the *Mystic*, transporting freight around New York Harbor. For the first extended period, Bram was home at night with his family. Apparently, Mr. Hottenroth had forgiven Bram over the restaurant business.

"When he came to us it was with the strongest kind of recommendations," recalled Manhattan Lighterage manager and partner Henry L. Joyce, "and he was an unusually competent man, having led a seafaring life for many years." Joyce got to know Bram well. As far as Joyce or fellow workers knew, Bram neither smoked nor drank. He volunteered at a local church and belonged to a

Masonic lodge. He "was a fine looking man . . . and had a splendid physique," said Joyce, noting also that Bram was "scrupulously neat and well dressed . . . away above the average river man." He was as well "way above the average as regards intelligence . . . and we always found him a sober, industrious and trustworthy man."

The company had no complaints about Bram—"we never had an accident or lost a dollar through carelessness or incompetency while Bram was in command" of the *Mystic*—but elements of his character were noted. "He certainly was a queer man and we who thought we knew him were continually surprised by him." Bram's greatest fault, as Joyce saw it, was that he "talked entirely too much for his own good. He was full of plans and schemes and many people [thought] he was demented." Bram would bring into the office a full set of ship plans that he had drawn and discuss details with Joyce, but Bram "seemed despondent" because he wasn't making money fast enough to build his ship. Eventually, he "became money-mad, and morning, noon and night he talked of nothing but money and his ship."

The engineer of Bram's lighter came to Joyce concerned that Bram frequently walked the deck for a whole morning, speaking to no one, apparently lost in thought. Joyce wasn't concerned: "I didn't speak to Bram at all [about it], because he was doing his work well, and that was all I cared about."

Joyce also didn't care about Bram's heritage. "He used to say that he was a Nova Scotian but we knew he was a half-bred St. Kitts negro. He was very sensitive on this point, however, and the men on the river never had much to say when Bram got talking about his nationality." Whenever he could, in conversation or minor documents, Bram portrayed himself as a white man from Nova Scotia, where his mother supposedly still lived. On important government and legal documents, Bram gave his proper birthplace, but when the form asked for race he always wrote "white." From natural appearance and the weathering of a nautical life, he could pass, and this satisfied him and most others. His wife and in-laws assumed he was white. The three Bram boys had much more of their mother's coloring, and no one questioned their racial heritage.

None of the odd aspects of Bram's character had anything to do with his departure from the lighterage company in June 1895. Business had slowed, and Bram was to be laid off for a few weeks. Instead, he decided to resign right away and go back to sea. Later, some newspapers reported that Bram left the job "under a cloud"; this Joyce "empathically" denied.

Early in the morning on July 1, Bram left his house in Brooklyn and went to his in-laws' house. Mrs. Hottenroth said, "he came to me and asked me for money. . . . He told me that he wanted to provide a flat for Hattie, but I didn't believe him." She refused to give him money, and he left. Later that day, Hattie got a letter from him saying he had lost his job and "gone to sea to make some money." Six months later, having heard nothing from him, Hattie initiated divorce proceedings on the grounds of desertion. She deposed that Bram had first left her six years earlier, returned after two years, and then left again the previous July.

Bram somehow got wind of Hattie's divorce intentions and sent her a letter in March 1896 saying that "he had not deserted her, that he never meant to do so, and that he was coming home to look after her and the children." But he did not come back, leaving his family impoverished. The children were for a time placed in the care of a Brooklyn charity, and Hattie, through the efforts of a sympathetic Joyce, got a job as a cleaner at the Metropolitan Opera House in Manhattan. The divorce was not consummated. "Mr. Bram is married and has three children," his lawyer would later say. "His family live in Brooklyn, but there have been domestic difficulties . . . and he is not now and has not for some time been living with his family."

Bram returned to the sea in July 1895. He shipped as second mate on the barkentine *White Wings*, sailing from New York to

Brazil, with a scheduled return to Baltimore. Bram, though, got off the ship in Rio to join a British steamship, the *Manin*, as second mate in early February 1896. The ship went first to Buenos Aires, loading grain and livestock, and then crossed the Atlantic to Liverpool, where Bram left the ship in early May and sought another ship back to the United States.

"I have found him thoroughly competent and trustworthy and a perfectly sober & steady officer," *Manin* captain George Cruse attested in an affidavit about Bram's service. "I have great pleasure in recommending him to anyone requiring his services."

To get back to Boston as quickly as possible, Bram shipped a week after arriving in Liverpool as a regular crewman on a steamer and arrived in Boston in late May.

In Boston, he had neither time nor money to see his family in Brooklyn. He set about looking for a ship. As it happened, a man who had been slated to be first mate on the *Herbert Fuller* backed out before he signed on, deciding instead to take the same position on a schooner anticipating a much shorter voyage.

On June 9, Bram and Captain Charles Nash met for the first time. Bram had been recommended to Nash by the US shipping commissioner in Boston and by Edward Parker, who was connected with McIntyre's ship chandlery in Boston. Parker said that Bram had been on several vessels fitted out by McIntyre and "had given complete satisfaction." Nash demanded of Bram a detailed account of his shipping life and supporting documents. Bram provided testimonials from Cruse, Brett, and other employers. A Boston shipping master who knew him, W. O. Wilson, averred that he was "a fine young man." Bram was hired. William Whicker, an assistant in Wilson's office who knew both Bram and Nash very well, later said that Nash "had a good deal of confidence in Bram," so much that as soon as he hired Bram as first mate at forty dollars a month, Nash left his ship in Bram's care for an extended visit home to Maine.

At seven in the morning on June 10, Bram boarded the *Herbert Fuller* at the East Boston Dry Dock. Two days later, the ship moved over to Mystic Wharf to begin loading pine boards bound for Argentina. In the weeks before sailing, Bram had general charge of the ship, while a stevedore had charge of the cargo loading. Nash apparently trusted completely his first mate's preparations. Bram lived aboard the ship; Nash mostly stayed ashore. Nothing in their initial relations suggested any sort of trouble.

3

CAST OF OTHER
CHARACTERS

Sailors are simple-minded men, as a rule; their mental
processes are elemental.

—Mary Roberts Rinehart, *The After House* (1914)

THE SHIP

The *Herbert Fuller*, built in 1890, was a wood-hulled barkentine, that is, a three-masted ship, with the foremast square-
rigged for downwind sailing and the main and mizzenmasts
fore-and-aft-rigged for performance upwind. The barkentine was
a very popular rig in the late 1890s, a time when steam was over-
taking sail on the world's commercial and passenger routes.

If it seems odd now to have launched a sailing ship in 1890,
it was not then. Nearly twice as many sail-powered as steam-
powered merchant vessels were then in service on the globe's
oceans: 21,000 against 11,000. But sail was in rapid decline and
steam in steady ascent. Seven years later, steam for the first time
outnumbered sail. In 1897, the *Journal of Commerce* reported 14,168
merchant sailing ships and 14,183 large merchant steamships, that

is, a considerable increase in steamships and a one-third decline in sailing ships during the decade. The rise of steam and the decline of sail accelerated in the years ahead.

Yet sail lingered. The number of new steamships built in the United States had increased gradually each decade of the 1800s, from none to 4,000 during the 1880s, but then dipped slightly during the next two decades. Meanwhile, the building of sailing ships, which peaked during the middle two decades of the 1800s at 12,000, declined nearly 40 percent during the next decade, then declined only gradually for the next three decades. During the first decade of the twentieth century, US shipbuilders produced roughly an equal number of new sail and steamships; during the 1890s, American yards produced 5,000 sailing ships and only 3,500 steamships. The first year of that decade produced the *Herbert Fuller*.

There were reasons sail hung on. Ships powered only by wind were (and are) cheaper to operate. Aside from sails being cheaper to make and repair than mechanical engines, especially at sea, wind is free, while engines cost money in fuel and lost cargo space and require more manpower than sails. Until steam technology produced more efficient and reliable engines in the opening decades of the twentieth century, sail for many builders and shippers remained a better option, especially as sailing ships transitioned from traditional square riggers to modified, efficient rigs like the brigantine. In ships, as in many things, the new makes a statement, the old adapts, and only gradually the old fades away while the new replaces it.

The *Herbert Fuller* was 158 feet long and 35 feet wide on her beam, with a draft of 18 feet. Her net tonnage was 742.79 tons. All in all, a modest vessel but suited to her times.

The building of the *Herbert Fuller* was overseen by her future captain Charles I. Nash. The Nash family of Harrington, Maine, turned out many sailing ships from the 1880s into the 1900s and made money at it. In 1890, Charles was thirty-six, one of dozens of

Harrington Nashes, in a town of a thousand people. Many other Harrington families were related to the Nashes through marriage. The *Fuller* was hardly a unique ship, but her builder-captain designed her with a particularly large, comfortable, high-roofed aft cabin or after house where he spent his time when not on deck. "There was not a stick of timber, or treenail in the vessel that he did not see before it was put in place."

CAPTAIN AND WIFE

Charles Nash was one of seven children, and the oldest son, of Alonzo P. and Emily Nash. Alonzo was descended from brothers Isaiah and Uriah Nash, the first settlers of the village of Harrington around 1804. The town of Harrington, midway between Bar Harbor and Machias, had been incorporated seven years earlier. Shipbuilding was the main industry of Harrington; many dozens of sailing ships were built in Harrington yards through the 1800s.

Among the several shipbuilding families, the Nashes were the most productive, turning out half of Harrington's ships. Alonzo Nash himself built twenty ships and, at age sixty in 1889, would have built more, but in his shipyard that June he was struck in the head by a wayward piece of timber and died a few days later. "He held various town offices," noted a brief obituary, "and was highly esteemed as a business man and as a citizen." His sons Charles, Wilbur, and Ernest continued building ships, taking some of them to sea themselves.

Charles was particularly attached to the *Herbert Fuller*, which was the last ship he built. His voyages in her were mostly up and down the Atlantic Seaboard, often carrying lumber. Among the captain's many voyages before his final voyage were several of note.

On December 27, 1893, a schooner, the *Levanter* of Thomaston, Maine, making her way north from Brunswick, Georgia, to New York with a load of lumber, had ventured too close to Cape

Hatteras when a gale came up. The ship, with captain E. N. Bunker, the captain's wife, their twelve-year-old son, and nine men, foundered. "It was the same old story," scolded one of the many papers reporting the story, "of trying to breast Cape Hatteras in the teeth of a fierce gale." The sails were torn away, waves battering the wooden hull ripped away planking beneath the waterline, lifeboats were smashed by boarding seas, and the 644-ton ship, flooded to her decks, settled in for a sinking. The twelve people aboard lashed themselves to the top of the aft cabin, ten feet above deck, and waited until the waterlogged cargo and hull finally lost their buoyancy, the ship broke apart, or another vessel sighted them.

For nearly three days, they waited, freezing and with a few biscuits and a gallon jug of water the captain brought up before the boat foundered. Hunger, thirst, and exposure threatened to kill them if they didn't drown first. "We all lay huddled together, my boy in my arms," recalled Mrs. Bunker. "At daylight, when we revived, none could relate how he spent the night." With daylight on the twenty-eighth, "the men sat up to look around for a sail, and saw none [and] the very heart left them all. God only knows how we passed that day, that night, the next day and the next night." Finally, at noon on the thirtieth, after two and a half days lashed to the deckhouse, sails appeared on the southern horizon: the *Herbert Fuller*, making the same passage from Georgia to New York, but a more seamanly hundred miles farther to the east. As luck would have it, this was precisely to where, as the wind had backed from northeast to northwest, the *Levanter* had drifted. Up went signals that the *Fuller* had spotted the *Levanter* and her people. "Their hearts leaped with joy at the approaching end of their sufferings, though they could scarcely move in their benumbed condition to give expression to it."

The storm that wrecked the *Levanter* had passed, but a heavy sea was still running. Over seven hours, three difficult trips in a boat from the *Fuller* succeeded in rescuing everyone, the captain's wife and son among the first, Captain Bunker appropriately among the last. Many of the men were badly frostbitten but grateful to be alive. They were given dry clothing and warm food. Mrs. Bunker and her son were given Nash's cabin. The *Fuller* arrived four days later in New York, where news of the rescue spread from the waterfront to newspaper offices. "Capt. Nash is quite modest in speaking of his part in the rescue," reported the *World*, "but Capt. Bunker never tires in his praise."

Five months later, an entirely different opinion of Captain Nash emerged, from his own crew. "The men assert . . . that the captain cursed them and threatened that not a single one of them should leave the ship alive." This six-man crew, to a man different from the crew that participated in the *Levanter* rescue, "say it was for his brutal conduct largely that they refused to obey him." The *Fuller*, this time sailing with coal from Philadelphia down Delaware Bay and out into the ocean to Boston, had put in at Lewes, Delaware, on May 28. The following morning, the crew refused to weigh anchor; they also "demanded butter on their bread for breakfast," claimed an outraged Nash, who considered them mutinous. The men, four Americans and two Swedes, were taken off to jail for court proceedings in June; within a fortnight, they were all released without charge. "While Capt. Nash has a most excellent reputation among men of his craft and . . . shipping agents and brokers," he could also be rough, "and upon this particular occasion his treatment of his men was said to have been harsh." When the crew threatened to go over the ship's rail at Lewes, Nash had told them, "Only corpses go over that rail." A new crew was sent from Philadelphia, and the voyage soon continued. The incident shows that relations between master and men on the *Herbert Fuller* were not always harmonious and sometimes dangerous. The *Fuller* was hardly unique in this. The same day that the *Fuller*'s crew mutinied, a schooner's crew in Philadelphia was arrested after they "objected to the mate's too frequent and generous use of 'cuss' words and of their general ill-treatment."

The *Fuller* voyage just prior to its most infamous one was also troubled. The fact seems to be that Nash "was very brusk [*sic*] in his manner," said Jonathan Spencer, the steward of the *Fuller* on its final two voyages. On this voyage, starting in late 1895 from New York to Martinique, Apalachicola, and Boston, the captain had "a number of differences" with his first mate. Spencer "heard the captain call him a dutch ___ at the supper table, and they had a hot time over it." In Martinique, the mate took the ship's boat ashore without express permission from Nash, who upon the mate's return told him permission was required. The mate said he thought it was his right to do so as first officer, and "they got hot over it." Then there was a disagreement over scrubbing the deck, and Nash sent the mate down to the aft cabin, where Nash "got the mate by his throat and tried to make him apologize." On a third occasion, Spencer saw Nash "pick up a broom handle and raise it above the mate as if to strike him." "There is no doubt" that Nash was "a very gruff man," said Spencer, "a man who would run for his revolver on the slightest provocation." But never with the regular crew: "It always seemed to be with the mates."

Opinion varied on this. To Johnny Ostergren, a well-regarded sailor who served on the *Fuller* for seven months from 1891 to 1892, Nash was "one of the most cordially disliked shipmasters sailing deep water vessels." Ostergren "never knew a crew to contract to go on the Fuller a second time after the experiences of one voyage." Still, as bad as Nash was with his crews—denying shore leave, calling all hands to work ship in calm weather—he was worse with the mates. In Pernambuco, said Ostergren, Nash beat the second mate for getting drunk ashore; after another, minor, infraction, the two prepared for a fistfight on deck when "the captain called his wife, and she came up on deck, crying. 'Get my biggest revolver,' he said. 'You don't want your revolver,' she replied." He insisted and she got it. The mate dared Nash to shoot, and he did: "The bullet just grazed the mate's head and went tearing through the cabin and settled in a bulkhead."

Nash was built for the rough physical life aboard sailing ships. He was five feet, nine inches tall and two hundred pounds, with brown hair and a large brown mustache. In all, a stocky man with a physical and mental presence equal to the challenge of his surroundings, or nearly so.

There was a time when the most famous Ray from Harrington, Maine, was Irving Burton "Stubby" Ray. Stubby Ray was a star baseball player at the University of Maine and then played a few years in the major leagues, as a shortstop for the Boston Beaneaters (today's Atlanta Braves) and the Baltimore Orioles. Ray survives on an obscure line in the record books. In 1888, he played a game at shortstop for twelve innings and didn't touch a ball—no putouts, no assists, no errors: a record for doing nothing. He was long retired and running a Boston grocery in 1896 when his older sister Laura sailed from Boston with her husband for the last time and soon surpassed Stubby as Harrington's most notable Ray.

Laura Agnes Ray was born in Harrington on December 2, 1857, the first of three children of Adoniram Ray, a master ship joiner and occasional captain, and his wife, Livonia A. Nash, of the other prominent family of Harrington. Harrington then was booming, with eighteen shipbuilders employing the greatest portion of the community. A century later, the population was half and shipbuilding was a memory. Today, the population has rebounded somewhat, though all the shipyards, Rays, and Nashes are long gone.

Laura and Charles were children together on the same Harrington street. Her father died in 1877, at fifty-six. Three years later, Laura and Charles married. She had little desire to stay home while her husband sailed long voyages, so she often traveled with him. It was not unusual for wives from seafaring backgrounds to do so; in the Nashes' case, it was made easier as the couple produced no children. If husband or wife was disappointed by this, neither told. If there was a biological explanation, neither likely knew. If there was a more personal explanation, it went unsaid.

At thirty-eight, Laura Nash was full bodied and attractive; she was, said a captain who knew the Nashes well, "a brunette, and very entertaining." As disliked as her husband may have been by some of the men who sailed with him, Laura Nash "was a splendid woman and perfectly ladylike and quiet," said a former crew member, "and all the men liked her. There never was a whisper about her in the forecastle."

THE CREW

There was a substantial change in the general composition of the *Fuller*'s crews during the 1890s. In 1893, when the ship made a daring rescue and experienced a minor mutiny, the crew was mostly American born; three years later, it entirely was not. This reflected a change that was taking place on most American sailing ships in the late 1800s. In 1885, a third of seamen who shipped in Massachusetts for coastwise voyages were American citizens; by 1900, it was only one in ten. American seamen were switching to steam vessels or quitting the sea entirely. American sailing ships increasingly were going to sea with European sailors, who tended to follow orders with the limited English they knew and brought a more traditional respect for the rules of a ship where the captain, for better or worse, was the law. For non-American sailors, service on American ships was a path to American naturalization and citizenship that many of them desired, whether they wanted to rise to mates or even captains, which required American citizenship, or to seek the benefits of citizenship ashore.

While ship crews in earlier generations were famously mistreated and ill paid, by the approach of the twentieth century government regulation and oversight ensured generally decent treatment. Various incidents notwithstanding, the crews of the *Herbert Fuller* were generally well treated, well fed, and paid prevailing wages or better. From 1891 to early 1896, the monthly wages for the *Fuller*'s first mate increased from thirty to fifty dollars, for the second mate from twenty to thirty dollars, and for seamen generally from twelve to twenty dollars, all in line with prevailing rates for the period.

For the voyage starting from Boston in July 1896, the crew consisted of two mates and six sailors, none of the eight American born. The day before the *Fuller* sailed from Boston, Charles Nash met his younger brother Ernest at a shipbroker's office. "What kind of a crew have you got, Charlie?" asked Ernest, himself a captain. "Very good, I think," said Charles. They "appear to be all right. Guess they'll do." This was the brothers' final conversation.

———⋘⋙———

AUGUST W. BLOMBERG, as second mate, was head of the ship's starboard watch. Among all the people aboard, the least is known about Blomberg. He was a Russian Finn by birth, date unclear; five foot, ten inches tall; and large bodied, larger even than his burly captain. To his fellow crew members, Blomberg was mostly known as Mr. Blume or Blum, an indication that on working ships a man's position mattered more than his name. The newspapers would regularly misname him: Blandberg, Brandberg, Banberg, Blembery, or Banberry. The *New York Times*, not quite yet the newspaper of record, opted for Blanberg. The *Boston Globe* reported his hometown as Bjorneberg, that his parents were poor, that he had followed the sea since he was "a small lad," that he had come to America in 1893 with the promise to his "attractive and robust" Finnish sweetheart that he would send for her when he made good, that making second mate on the *Fuller* was a great step in that direction, and that his name was Bamberg.

Eventually, this all settled down, alternately and wrongly at first, to Blamberg or Bramberg, and finally correctly to Blomberg.

Regardless, he was described as "a thorough and reliable seaman" who had been a naturalized American citizen. He may well have been, though the record of this is not readily found.

Before his *Herbert Fuller* voyage, Blomberg drank. Spencer saw him drunk "lying on the floor" outside the ship's carpentry shop the morning they left the dock, but "I never see him drunk after we got to sea."

———————⧓———————

IN BLOMBERG'S STARBOARD watch were Folke Wassen, Oscar Anderson, and Henry J. Slice: a Russian Finn in charge of two Swedes and a German on an American ship bringing New England pine to Argentina.

Wassen was twenty-one, born in Gothenburg. He'd been at sea on a variety of ships as an ordinary seaman for three years. This made him, among the *Fuller*'s sailors, both the oldest to have first gone to sea and the youngest among them. It was somewhat unusual that after three years as an ordinary seaman, he had not earned promotion to able seaman, which brought better wages. One to two years was the average before promotion; why after three years Wassen had not moved up is unknown. Wassen boarded the *Fuller* on July 3, the day she sailed. He, like every member of the crew, had not sailed before with any other crew member. Wassen "spoke very little English." There is no record of Wassen in America after the trials; apparently, he returned to Sweden and lived out his days unremarkably.

Like Wassen, Oscar Anderson was a Swede. As a young boy, he'd had some training at massage, but he'd been a sailor since age fourteen; by the time he boarded the *Herbert Fuller* as an able seaman, he had been at sea for eleven years on "pretty near all kinds of vessels." Anderson would be naturalized as an American citizen in 1897. By then, he had some schooling in physiology, anatomy, and massage, "with a view of earning my living by some other means than by following the sea." He soon found work as a rubber at Boston City Hospital and then as a massager at the Butler Exercise Club, on the top floor of the five-story building at 309 Washington Street, generally known as the Record Building, for the *Boston Evening Record*, which occupied the main floor. By 1902, Anderson was the manager of the club; he would retain that position until his death in 1925. In 1899, he married a Swedish-born woman, Anna; he was twenty-eight, she thirty-two. They had several children. When he died, Anderson was regarded as a "prominent masseur" of Boston and Medford, where the family lived and Anna was active in charitable affairs. By all accounts, the family was happy, though for whatever reason, possibly to avoid late or early commutes, Anderson sometimes spent the night in an apartment attached to the club. On the night of October 5, 1925, a Monday, Anderson went to bed at the club and did not wake up. A friend discovered the body, robed, the following morning. Anderson's death was "believed due to natural causes."

Henry Slice was born in Hamburg, Germany, around 1865. At age sixteen, he went to sea as an ordinary seaman, advancing to able seaman after two years, a typical period. After a decade or so at sea on a variety of ships, he was naturalized as an American citizen in Jersey City. By the time of his *Herbert Fuller* voyage, Slice, a compact five foot six and 160 pounds, had sailed on all types of vessels. After the trials, he worked as a porter for American Express—then, as it had been founded, a shipping company—at the North Union train station (the site now of North Station).

In 1901, Slice boarded with a family in Charlestown; his landlady said he "had good habits" and was always home when he wasn't at work. He never married. On August 31 of that year, a Saturday, he finished work at three in the afternoon and disappeared. Henry Slice was never seen again. In 1937, a longtime inmate at a Massachusetts poor farm who went by "John Brown" died. He left no will or other document indicating his true identity. He had "stubbornly denied" what some people thought: that he was Henry Slice. For whatever reason, he wanted no association with Slice, crewman of the *Herbert Fuller*.

As FIRST MATE, Bram had charge of the port watch, with three men under him. Hendrik "Henry" Albert Perdok was born in Holland in 1874 and left school for the sea at age twelve. Over the next decade, he shipped on "brigantines, barkentines, barks and a couple of steamers." He arrived in an American port for the first time only fourteen days before he shipped on the *Herbert Fuller*. Not surprisingly, "I could not understand so much English at that time," nor did he even understand the difference between first and second mates. But he was a quick study. After his *Herbert Fuller* voyage and its long aftermath, he settled in Fitchburg and by 1903, at a meeting of the local chapter of the Royal Arcanum, had given a "thrilling" talk on his experiences. "Mr. Perdok's love of the sea is yet strong," reported the local paper, "but for trouble with his eyesight, he would have been now a sailor."

Instead, he became a fireman, married a French Canadian, and with her had four children: a boy who died young and three daughters who never married. His wife, Genevieve, reason unknown, left the family home "without just cause" in 1916 and died the following year. Around that time, Perdok moved to New Bedford, where he died in 1952, age seventy-seven. The brief Associated Press obituary noted that Perdok was on watch at the time of the murders fifty-five years earlier but failed to note that he was the last survivor of the *Herbert Fuller*. One of his daughters, Stella, lived for ninety-seven years and died in 2004, the last direct relative of any of the July 1896 crew of the *Herbert Fuller*.

Francis "Frank" Loheac was born in September 1871, in Landré-varzec, a small village in Brittany, "the part of France that makes sailors." He had gone to sea at thirteen and sailed on steamers and sailing vessels of "every kind: barks, schooners, barkentines." He had also served in the French navy for a period that was not quite as long as was required of him: "I have left my country without authorization, and I am liable to be punished if I am caught by them."

He first arrived in the United States just before his twenty-first birthday; from then, when not at sea, he resided in Boston. Apparently alone among the *Fuller* crew, he had sailed before to Rosario, though not from Boston. Loheac and Wassen were the only crew members acquainted with each other before the voyage: they had met at a boardinghouse where they each stayed in the several days prior to sailing. Loheac applied for US citizenship in 1897; he was naturalized in 1899. For a few years, he was a streetcar conductor and then a clerk in Boston; in the late 1910s, he worked on fishing boats out of Pensacola, Florida, where he then lived. In 1920, he lied to the US Census that his parents had been Canadian and that he had been born in Nova Scotia. Eventually, he migrated back north to Staten Island, where he died in 1942. He never married and had no children. His life passed without attracting much attention, perhaps by design.

The remaining sailor of the port watch was Justus Leopold Westerberg, the oldest and strangest sailor aboard. He was born in May 1855 in Sweden and went to sea at seventeen. He first touched an American shore in 1883 but remained a Swedish citizen for many more years. In 1884, when shipping from Quebec on an English ship, the boarding master suggested a remedy for the sailor's mouthful of a name. "When you go aboard the ship and the captain asks you what your name is, tell him Charley Brown." The name stuck. By 1896 he had been second mate for ten years mostly on Nova Scotian ships and occasionally a first mate. On the *Fuller* he was again just a crewman.

Brown née Westerberg was short—five foot five—but muscular and well built, with blue eyes, a "pleasant" and open face, and a substantial blond mustache. "His manner," in the opinion of one close observer, "was that of a seafaring man who had ceased to expect luck." In fact, he had had some very bad luck, on July 12, 1891, five years plus a day before the trouble on the *Fuller*.

Brown had just completed a long voyage on a Nova Scotian ship—from Philadelphia to Japan to Tacoma to Antwerp—and planned to visit some of his brothers and sisters who then lived in Copenhagen. He took a train from Antwerp to Rotterdam, intending to take a ferry from there to Copenhagen, but on the train began to feel sick. "I commenced getting scared of everybody I see around me. . . . I thought they were going to do me some harm, steal my money." Brown had with him fifty-five pounds, for him the very substantial pay in wages from his long voyage. Arriving in Rotterdam, he managed to get a room in a lodging house and tried to sleep. A man appeared at his door, and Brown, with a pistol he carried, shot at him. The bullet missed its target and shattered a window. Police came, and Brown, who had passed out, was sent to a hospital, where it took him two weeks to regain his senses, but not his money, which had disappeared. He remembered nothing of the shooting, only what he was told about it. A few days later, fully recovered and having caused no injuries to anyone, he was released from the hospital without charges. Soon, he was back at sea, and given to telling and embellishing his shooting story. "I used to spin lots of yarns. I tell Frank [Loheac] lots of stories." In fact, in the opening days of his *Fuller* voyage, he told his crewmates that he had shot and killed a man in Rotterdam. It is unclear if his crewmates believed him.

Brown had arrived in Boston in late May 1896 as first mate on a British ship from Calcutta. "He was a very quiet, peaceable old fellow and wouldn't harm a mosquito," said Peter Swansen, the keeper of a Boston sailors' boardinghouse who shipped Brown on the *Fuller*. Brown, "almost a simpleton," had worked for Swansen in the preceding weeks, "and I would be glad to trust my life to him." After his voyage on the *Herbert Fuller* and its aftermath, Brown was naturalized as an American citizen (under his birth name) and went back to sea. In 1907, though, he was again in a Swedish hospital, where he attacked his nurse with a knife. The nurse survived, but Brown was certified criminally insane; he remained confined until his death in 1920.

THE STEWARD

Like his *Fuller* shipmates, Jonathan Spencer had been at sea for many of his years, shipping first as a cabin boy at fourteen ten years earlier and eventually serving on a variety of ships as steward. He was the only person aboard the *Fuller* who knew the Nashes before their final voyage. Spencer had joined their ship in New York in December 1895, for that long voyage delivering general cargo to Martinique; then timber to Apalachicola, Florida; and different timber to Boston. Otherwise, he was like everyone else on board: a stranger to every other.

Spencer was black; unlike Bram, who insisted against all evidence on his whiteness, Spencer's racial identity was no issue. He was born on St. Vincent in 1872—the month varies from one official document to the next—and first arrived at an American port, Philadelphia, in 1888, though he did not become a naturalized American citizen until 1917. He was of average height (five feet and eight and a half inches) and eventually comfortable weight (two hundred pounds) and at some point acquired, as many sailors do, tattoos, of unknown design, on both hands. Spencer's life at sea as steward afforded him a certain freedom. He kept his own hours as required to maintain the ship's galley, prepare meals, and, in the aft cabin, make up beds and keep things tidy. Spencer liked this role, preferring to be considered the ship's steward, not merely its cook, though the crew with whom he quartered in the forward cabin valued him only as the man who fed them.

As steward and cook, Spencer didn't keep watches or help with the sailing of the ship, but he had served on many—barkentines, schooners, and barks. In between voyages, Brooklyn was his home, 275 Bergen Street. The building is long gone; the address is now home to a New York City food-stamp center. At the time of the *Fuller* voyage from Boston in 1896, Spencer had been married for two years, and his wife, Josephine, from Barbados, was pregnant. Their only child, Louise, would eventually gain a bit of public notice in the 1920s as a soprano, performing with her husband, Ulric Hassell, a saxophone player and bandleader, at concerts for Marcus Garvey. The marriage ultimately failed; Louise died in 1965.

Her father, meanwhile, remained a steward, shipping all over the world until 1942, when he was sixty-nine years old. Two years earlier, he became the steward on the American freighter *Isabela*. The ship, headed from New York to Puerto Rico, was off the coast of Haiti late in the morning of May 19, 1942, when it was torpedoed and sunk by a German U-boat. Thirty-four survivors in two lifeboats made it to a Haitian beach; three crew members went down with the ship, Jonathan Spencer apparently among them. He had spent more than a half century on ships and died on one without any notice of his passing.

IT WAS NOT strange that among the hired hands on the *Herbert Fuller* few bothered to introduce themselves to each other. It is typical on ships. After nearly six days at sea, Spencer heard a conversation between "Loheac and that old sailor, I don't know his name." He meant Brown. "I think his name is Harris," Spencer said of Henry Slice, whose first name Spencer thought was Harry; as to the rest, "I don't know their names." Spencer knew Folke

Wassen only as "the young fellow." Until the seventh day, Spencer "never had any conversation with any of the sailors." Until then, Perdok didn't know Bram's name; he just called the mate "sir." Bram called Loheac "Loheez." As to Wassen, "I don't believe I said two words to him on board the ship. . . . [A]ll the time he was there, I never spoke with him." As far as Lester Monks knew, Blomberg's name was Blume, Bram's was Brown, and Brown wasn't called by any name.

If he wasn't sure of their names, Monks did hold certain opinions about his shipmates. "The crew speak very little English," Monks wrote in a private journal. "The Dutchman [presumably Perdok] has the lowest intelligence of any man I have ever seen. The mate sent him aft for a broom and the Dutchman rolled down into the cabin. As the first mate is only in the cabin while eating meals you can imagine the effect the Dutchman produced in the cabin."

Bram and Spencer did get acquainted before the *Fuller* sailed. Spencer remembered quite clearly Bram's first comments on the Nashes. Laura had gone ashore and returned in a new dress. "Calico makes a great change with a woman," Bram said to Spencer. "Why, yes," Spencer replied. What either man was thinking is not recorded.

For this voyage, as many previous, the *Fuller* was loaded with lumber. "Both holds, the lower hold and 'tween decks was filled right up," Bram would later explain. "We had also . . . a deck load with a height of fully five feet." The deck was loaded with five feet of lumber all the way from the forward end of the forward house to the forward end of the after house, flush with its height, and then two and a half feet high on either side of the house to its aft end, just under the cabin windows. For its greatest part, the deck load effectively became the deck, and a new railing was fashioned above it. Such loading was typical for a ship carrying lumber, though the *Fuller*'s lumber deck would became a stage of sorts, a scene setting in a most atypical and unwanted drama.

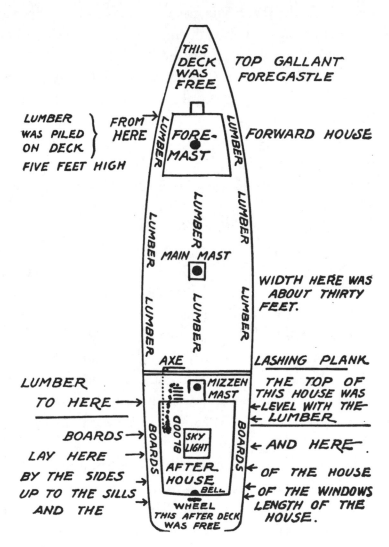

ROUGH SKETCH OF THE DECK.

From *The Green Bag*, vol. 9, no. 4 (April 1897)

4

LIFE AND DEATH
ON BOARD

The murderer is a go-getter. The murderer has a problem and he solves it. The murderer sees what he wants,
and he takes it. The murderer believes in quick action:
he is a maker of success: he is a man with *results*.

—"Murder as Bad Art,"
New Yorker, September 19, 1925

M onks boarded the *Herbert Fuller* at ten thirty on the evening
of July 2, a Thursday. A couple of friends got him settled
and left. One was not especially close. His full name was William
Oakey, "as far as I know," Monks later said, and may have lived in
Dorchester. Phillip Dumaresq, on the other hand, was a Brookline
neighbor and a Harvard classmate; his father, Frank, was a longtime friend and Harvard classmate of Lester's uncle George.

The night was hot and Monks didn't sleep. His room was
hardly luxurious and poorly ventilated. It had a sleeping bunk that
ran the length of the room, floor space the size of the bunk, no
closets or other cabinetry other than locker drawers underneath
the bunk, and one window.

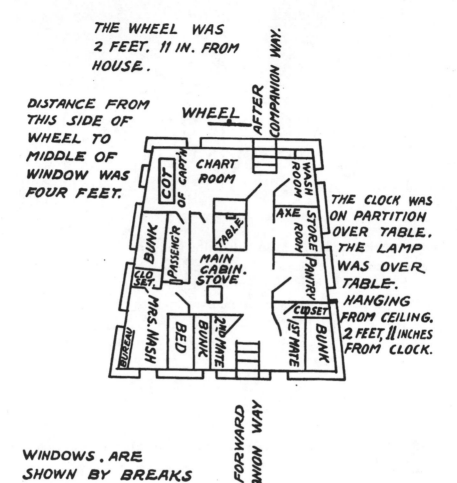

THE WHEEL WAS 2 FEET. 11 IN. FROM HOUSE.

DISTANCE FROM THIS SIDE OF WHEEL TO MIDDLE OF WINDOW WAS FOUR FEET.

WHEEL

AFTER COMPANION WAY.

CHART ROOM

COT OF CAPT'N

WASH ROOM

AXE

STORE ROOM PANTRY

THE CLOCK WAS ON PARTITION OVER TABLE. THE LAMP WAS OVER TABLE. HANGING FROM CEILING. 2 FEET, 11 INCHES FROM CLOCK.

BUNK

PASSENG'R

TABLE

MAIN CABIN. STOVE

CLO SET.

MRS. NASH

BUREAU

BED

BUNK

2ND MATE

CLOSET

1ST MATE

BUNK

FORWARD COMPANION WAY

WINDOWS. ARE SHOWN BY BREAKS IN OUTSIDE LINES.

LENGTH. OF AFTER HOUSE = 29 FEET.

ROUGH SKETCH OF THE AFTER HOUSE INSIDE.

From *The Green Bag*, vol. 9, no. 4 (April 1897)

Monks's room was the middle of three rooms that made up the starboard side of the aft cabin. The cabin was twenty-nine feet long, slightly less than that wide at its forward end and tapering aft by several feet. Its ceiling rose roughly five feet above the deck, and its floor was set two feet below the deck.

Just forward of Monks's room was the considerably larger room—roughly nine feet square—of Laura Nash. This room had two windows, one facing starboard, the other forward, the latter offering only small amounts of light and air on this voyage because the deck cargo of wood boards was stacked high and close. The main door for Mrs. Nash's room opened onto the common area of the cabin, which featured a stove for heat and the dining table. Mrs. Nash's room and the one occupied by Lester Monks were joined by a doorway, which usually made the two rooms a suite of sorts for the Nashes. On this voyage, the door between Mrs. Nash's room and Lester Monks's room was locked, from her side. It had been locked in advance of Monks's arrival and would remain so. As this door served no purpose for him, Monks placed his luggage against his side of it.

Monks's access to his room was via a door at the aft end of the room opening into the large chart room that formed the aft starboard corner of the after house. In the chart room, twelve feet across and nine and a half feet long, the captain did his navigating and, for this voyage, slept, on a small cot beneath two windows on the starboard side. Whether the sleeping arrangements—the Nashes separated by a third party—were something that had happened before is unknown. Incredibly, the question would never be asked—how it was that the only woman on board slept separated from her husband, with logistics making intimacy unlikely for the duration of the intended long voyage. The sleeping arrangement of husband and wife separated by a young man in close quarters for many weeks seems a design for trouble.

In addition to its two starboard-facing windows, the chart room also had a window facing aft; like all of the after house's windows, it measured sixteen inches long by eleven inches high with rounded corners and had sturdy vertical iron bars on the outside, to protect the glass. The center of the window was four feet from the closest spokes of the ship's wheel. Much would be made later about whether a person at the wheel could look through this window and see people in the chart room. Spencer, having completed one long prior voyage aboard, knew the ship best after its captain and was clear: "You couldn't see anything, standing at the wheel looking through the window." He recalled one time in particular, when the ship was being moved across the Hudson the previous December: "I stood at the wheel moving from Jersey to New York. Mrs. Nash was down in the cabin and I was steering the vessel with two tugs beside of her, and Mrs. Nash said something to me and I tried to look through the very same window and see her, and I couldn't see her." The same again in the preparation for the current voyage: "Moving from Mystic Dock to Long Wharf before we went on this voyage I have done the same thing and I couldn't see anything," insisted Spencer. "Mrs. Nash came up the after companionway and was asking something to me, and then she went down in the cabin and I looked again and I couldn't see her."

The chart room had three doorways: one into what for this voyage was the passenger's room, one right next to that one into the common area of the main cabin, and one along the room's aft wall onto the passageway leading to the aft companionway.

The chart room also had a writing desk, bookshelves, and a small organ that Laura Nash was known to play.

Continuing counterclockwise from Mrs. Nash's room was the second mate's room. The room was only the length of his bunk, about six feet, and about four and a half feet wide, about half of that being the bunk itself. A door, opening into the room, led to a short passageway that led to the forward companionway up to the deck. A window looked forward.

Opposite the second mate's room, on the other side of the companionway, was the first mate's room, at the port forward corner of the aft cabin. The room had a sizable bunk, with a window looking to port, plus a small closet at the aft end of the bunk. This made for open space extending for the length of the bunk plus the closet. The forward wall had a window looking forward.

Aft of the first mate's room was a large pantry, and aft of that the storeroom, with a spare bunk. The door to the storeroom from the main cabin opened next to the dining table. On the aft wall of the storeroom was the ship's axe. When the storeroom door was open, which it usually was, the axe was visible from the main cabin, especially to the two people who would sit on the port side of the dining table: Monks and Bram. The two people most familiar with the storeroom itself were Spencer, whose supplies were stored there, and Monks, whose beer and liquor were stored there. There was a window in the storeroom, looking out the port side of the ship. As regular crew were never in the aft cabin, the only people who could have known where the ship's axe was stored, aside from the Nashes and Blomberg, were Monks, Bram, and Spencer.

Aft of the storeroom at the port aft corner of the cabin was the lavatory. The door to the lavatory opened onto the passageway leading to the aft companionway; across the passageway was the door to the chart room.

The main room of the cabin, smaller than the chart room, had the stove forward and, projecting forward from the back wall, the dining table. From the ceiling above the table hung a lantern; on the wall aft of the dining table was the ship's clock. In order to see the clock and call the watch changes, the mates had to descend the forward companionway and look aft through the forward passageway and the main cabin.

Monks went ashore shortly after dawn on Friday, July 3, for breakfast, and met his father and brother, Archie, who came aboard for the tow down to Nantasket Roads, where the ship anchored to wait out easterly winds. Later in the day, Lester's uncle George came and left via steam launch. After supper, Lester turned in at eight in the evening, the hour in early July when night came (daylight savings time, proposed by a New Zealand scientist eight months earlier, wasn't adopted in the United States until 1918). Saturday, Independence Day, came in with heavy fog and still the easterly headwind. Monks bet Captain Nash a quarter the wind would shift by sunset. Nash was happy to take the bet and that evening collected his quarter.

Sunday the wind remained east, and Monday, too. "Still here with nothing to do but run on deck and look at compass," Monks recorded in his diary. The crew, meanwhile, were beginning to "feel badly" about having left the dock on a Friday, always a bad omen for superstitious seamen. True, they were still anchored at the harbor entrance, but the voyage had formally begun the previous Friday when the ship was towed from the dock. For the crew, the Friday departure was the reason for the persistent headwind that kept them anchored.

Tuesday also came in with fog and the easterly breeze, which gave Lester's mother and sister the opportunity for a final visit by small boat. At sunset the wind shifted to the west, and the fog lifted. Monks retired at nine but was woken at four the next morning by the sounds of the crew raising sails. A tug brought the ship out past the Boston lightship to open water. By noon, the *Herbert Fuller*, under full sail in a steady breeze, was out of sight of land.

Like every ship that goes to sea, the *Herbert Fuller* had two watches, in her case of four men apiece: the first mate and three seamen on the port watch, the second mate and the other three seamen on the starboard watch. "Starboard" for right on ships and the sea generally has been around for a millennia, arising from the Old English word for "steer" and indicating the side — board—for the placement then of the steering gear and the side of the boat from which to steer. The opposite was long called "larboard," the side from which boats generally were loaded when in port; only in the mid-1800s did larboard, which sounded too much like starboard, give way to the much more sensible "port."

On the *Herbert Fuller*, as on oceangoing vessels for many years before and since, watch service was four hours on, four hours off, with two two-hour "dog watches" to provide seven watch periods per day and alternating service each day. Thus, on day one, starting from noon, the port watch would be on until 4:00 p.m., off until 6:00 p.m., on until 8:00 p.m., off until midnight, on until 4:00 a.m., off until 8:00 a.m., and on until noon, thereby serving the alternate set of on and off watches for the next twenty-four hours. (Of course, on the *Fuller*, as on all ships, these times were rendered as hours on a twenty-four-hour clock.) On a long voyage especially, such as the two to three months anticipated by the *Herbert Fuller* on the departure for Argentina in early July 1896, this variation was designed to relieve some of the tedium. As it turned out, the *Fuller*'s crew experienced nothing like tedium.

From July 8, when the *Fuller* started sailing, until shortly before two in the morning on July 14, the voyage was entirely ordinary. There were periods of fog and some squalls, but the weather was mostly settled, typical for July in the Atlantic. The course steered was generally southeast, and the winds were generally light to moderate and from the west, pushing the ship along at six knots on average, sometimes slower, sometimes faster, with an added push of a knot or so from the Gulf Stream as it flowed east. There was no feeling aboard the ship that anything was amiss, nothing more than the usual tensions between people getting to know one another in the opening days of what everyone expected would be a long voyage.

The focus of social activity among the after house occupants, such as it was, was mealtimes at the dining table. The Nashes, Bram, and Monks took their meals together, attended by Spencer. Blomberg, on watch when Bram ate, took his meals separately. Conversation at table, it seems, was relatively minimal.

Monks and Nash established a literary relationship of sorts. Monks lent Nash his copy of a new Richard Harding Davis title, *Three Gringos in Venezuela and Central America*, an account of the American adventurer's recent travels. In exchange, Nash lent Monks *A Voyage to the Cape*, an 1886 account of a sea voyage taken by English writer William Clark Russell to ease his rheumatic gout. As a remediation, the voyage benefited Russell nothing, but the resulting memoir was popular. Among many true tales of the sea recounted in the book by Russell was the notorious recent mutiny on a large ship, the *Frank N. Thayer*, in the South Atlantic in which both mates and a number of sailors were murdered; the captain, Robert K. Clarke, with his wife and child aboard, was severely wounded but survived. In the last restful hours aboard the *Fuller*, Monks was particularly engrossed with Russell's detailed account.

During a dinner early in the voyage, according to Spencer, Laura Nash asked Monks what courses he took in college. "He told her he was studying medicine, or something like that." On deck later with Spencer, Bram was indignant: "Did you hear what she asked him?" Spencer said he had. "Any fool could ask that question," Bram continued. Spencer laughed, and Bram said, "She is only putting on. She is nothing but a factory girl." To this Spencer offered no response, perhaps knowing that she was not a factory girl but a social equal of her husband from their hometown.

It was suggested later that Laura Nash might have encouraged Lester Monks's attentions. Friends and family, though, who knew her from childhood said she could not have been "a voluntary cause of trouble on the ship." Her mind "was as pure as a girl's, and . . . she was the last woman in the world to rouse forbidden love in a man's heart. If she had suspected the mate [or anyone else] of entertaining too strong a regard for her she would have at once taken steps to avoid trouble." Still, there was the fact that she was thirty-eight and with her husband had created no family: "If she had any sorrow in life it was perhaps that their union had never been blessed with children."

Bram also had certain opinions about the captain, according to Spencer. "Has you got a good wife?" Bram asked. "Do you treat her well?"

Spencer said yes.

"Do you give her all she wants?"

"As far as my means allow me to do," Spencer replied.

And Bram said, "Here is a man that has got a good vessel, but don't take any care of her. He isn't deserving of her."

It is unclear if Bram meant the captain's wife or his ship.

Bram continued: "Some other sport would be pissing his money up against the wall."

Spencer agreed, and Bram said, "Captain Nash might die, and Mrs. Nash might get married to a young man, and that is just the way his money will go. Oh, I don't mean that way."

In Spencer's telling, it is hard to know just what Bram was getting at, if anything important beyond idle talk.

Though they took meals together, Bram and Monks had relatively little interaction. According to Monks, they had just one conversation during the first week of the voyage, when "I told him about my yachting experiences." Monks said Bram was dismissive: "I don't think he thought much of what he called fresh water sailors." In his diary, Monks noted that Bram was "a first rate navigator and very intelligent, but he gets but $40 month." Monks did not make clear whether he meant that forty dollars was under the going rate for first mates or that forty dollars seemed a pittance to him.

If relations in the aft cabin were muted, the relationship between the first and second mates seemed, to some of the crew, antagonistic. They had "high words" on deck the second day at sea and two days later an angry conversation outside the carpenter's shop in the forward cabin, overheard in parts by several crew members.

"That damn sarcastic talk of yours is the only thing I will kill a man for," Bram warned Blomberg, as Spencer heard it.

Blomberg gave an unheard reply, to which Bram sought to calm things: "Don't you get excited; don't you get excited."

Anderson heard Blomberg telling Bram, "Don't try to run me, I know my business . . . and you mind your own business." Brown claimed to hear something similar.

Loheac heard Blomberg say, "I wish you would let me go about my work," and that he'd served as mate on a ship with a crew of twenty-four, with which Bram was unimpressed: "I don't want to know where you have been or what you have done."

In all, four people heard different portions of the same conversations, or they heard the same conversations and remembered different parts of it. Three other crewmen—Wassen, Perdok, and Slice—observed the conversations on deck or below but couldn't quote them.

Wassen was at the wheel and only "heard them talk very loud . . . high words" on deck.

From up in the rigging, Slice saw the conversation and judged it "an argument" of which he couldn't hear the words.

Perdok heard the "loud" carpenter-shop conversation but "didn't understand so much English at the time."

In total, the supposed antagonism between the mates may have been nothing more than having "a growl once or twice," as Spencer put it, as the two men sorted out their shipboard relationship. Bram, on the other hand, would deny that the supposedly antagonistic conversation between him and Blomberg even took place.

At six on Monday the thirteenth, after supper, Nash and Laura, as was their routine, were walking arm in arm on the starboard side of the roof of the after house. This evening, Spencer observed Bram trying to speak to them. Nash apparently was not much interested in a conversation with his first mate. "The captain pointed a finger down to the deck and turned and walked off."

Bram looked at his retreating captain "from his head to his feet," then turned and walked away, approaching Spencer: "As soon as he got by me he said 'that ain't natural.'" These words were not spoken casually: "The man looked mad—you could see the words came from his heart by the expressions of his face." Yet "I don't know what he meant," said Spencer later.

Bram would never be asked to explain and never acknowledged that he said anything after what proved to be his final conversation with Nash.

"*That ain't natural.*" Had the captain asked his first mate to perform a task that the mate found offensive or beneath his station? Had the captain asked something stranger? Or did Bram say anything?

Monks, as was his habit after dinner, had come on deck to read. "Captain and Mrs. Nash were walking up and down on the deck house on the starboard side, and Mr. Bram came up, and spoke to them, and then went away." The space on top of the aft cabin was not large; words unless whispered, actions unless discreet, were heard and seen by all. Bram himself had no recollection of trying to engage the Nashes in conversation or the captain turning his back on him. Spencer was the only person who claimed to hear Bram's angry words. Maybe Bram said them, maybe he didn't; maybe Spencer heard, maybe he imagined, maybe he later invented.

Evening came. The Nashes went below first, followed by Monks at eight, just after sundown, each to their respective rooms. Spencer went forward to prepare the two mates' late supper—sandwiches that they ate during their respective nighttime watches—and then brought them to the aft cabin. Mrs. Nash was having trouble with the lamp over the table; Spencer helped her set it to a low blaze for the overnight and then went forward.

Bram stayed on deck with his watch until eight and then retired to his room. Blomberg had the deck with his watch. Slice steered for the first two hours, in the middle of which, around nine, a passing squall brought the captain on deck to talk briefly with his second mate. After a few minutes, Nash went below and fell asleep on his cot. Slice later said that, from the wheel looking through the window into the chart room, he could see the captain lying on his cot, just from his feet up to his knees. Wassen took over the wheel for the last two hours of the watch, from ten to midnight.

Toward the end of his shift, Wassen noticed that Blomberg, standing close by with his arms resting on top of the after house, seemed to have fallen asleep. Wassen "made a noise with my feet," and Blomberg woke and noticed it was midnight and the end of the starboard watch. Wassen gave the helm to Charley Brown of the oncoming port watch, and Blomberg went below without a word. Bram came up from the aft cabin and took his position in the middle of the ship; Perdok and Loheac came on deck from the forward cabin and took their positions forward.

The ship was headed southeast, and the breeze was moderate from the west, on the ship's starboard quarter; the sails, accordingly, were comfortably eased on the port side of the ship.

Having retired after sunset to his cabin that had no lantern, Monks, according to his account, went to bed quickly. He would also say that to prevent noise his door supposedly made when the ship rolled, as ships can do especially when the wind is on the quarter on the open sea, he closed and locked his door. He never said if this was a regular habit, to close and lock his door, or if he did so only this night because of the particular motion and resulting noise made by the door. There is only Monks's word that he closed and locked his door this night. Monks would say only that he did so. No one on the ship could prove that he did or didn't, and no one later asked him for details. Nothing is known of the door's construction or the locking mechanism; no tests were ever made. No one ever questioned Monks's assertion that he locked his door that night. It is extraordinary that nothing he did in the hours after he went to his room was ever seriously questioned, given what happened. "I used to lock it at night," he said. If that is true that he habitually locked it, then it is false that he said he locked it only on this night to prevent the door from squeaking with the motion of the ship.

LATE IN THE one o'clock hour on the morning of the fourteenth, four people were in their separate rooms in the aft cabin: Charles Nash, Laura Nash, August Blomberg, and Lester Monks. The ship was at 35.07 degrees latitude and 53.25 degrees longitude, a spot in the Atlantic determined by navigational calculation, not by any reference to land, the nearest of which was many hundreds of miles away. The Nashes and Blomberg were asleep; Monks later said he was too.

In that same hour, a man, quietly enough, made his way through the cabin and into the storeroom, where he took the ship's axe from the rear wall. He went first to Blomberg's room and struck the second mate with the axe eight, possibly nine, times. The first blow crushed a portion of his skull. It was enough to kill him. The other blows were to his head, jaw, collarbone, sternum, and left hand; the chop to the hand severed its little finger and thumb.

The killer moved through the cabin to its opposite corner, where he struck the sleeping captain seven times, all in the head, knocking him off his cot, which tipped on its side. Again, the first blow was enough to be fatal. Several times the axe blade went deep through the skull and into the captain's brain. Other blows penetrated the left eye and the upper and lower jaws.

Next, apparently after bypassing Monks's room, the killer entered Laura's and struck her eight, possibly nine, times. The first one or two blows struck her raised left arm and right hand; fingers were severed, the hand left hanging by a few tendons. Unlike the men who died asleep, Laura evidently had woken and been aware of her attacker and fate: her arm and hand wounds were defensive.

It is possible that she screamed, once. After the first blows, she succumbed to the rest without cognition. The axe, in its various transits, penetrated the right side of her head, crushed and smashed to pieces her upper and lower jaws, and struck her right breast. One head blow, whether intentional or not, was with the back of the axe, not the blade.

The men died on their backs; Laura Nash died on her left side, against the cabin wall, one leg straight out, the other bent, with her only garment, a light nightdress, up to her knees. The attacker wounded all three people so severely in their heads that, when the bodies eventually were examined, their skulls had drained: they "had no brains at all, they were empty."

The murderer was not perfect in his swing. Twice the axe cut wood over the second mate's door. Multiple times the axe blade struck the ceiling beam over the captain's cot. A cut in the ceiling in Laura Nash's room was likely made by more than one swing.

This made for a total of nearly thirty swings with the axe. It suggests a killer who was not in a hurry, redundantly effective in his purpose, if not perfect in his practice. His victims weren't just killed; they were thoughtfully and thoroughly mutilated. The killer, in taking his time in a place with no escape, was also seemingly confident about not being discovered, or perhaps he was unconscious of that concern.

Why he killed was not evident, though the redundancy suggests that the act of killing, not its effect, was primary: the killings were not a means to an end, but the end in themselves, the satisfaction of an urge. "The hands of a part of mankind have ever been set against their fellows," observed prolific mystery writer Melville Davisson Post six weeks earlier, in the foreword to his first book, "for what great reason no man can tell."

For what reason the *Herbert Fuller* killer killed, he never said. Who he was has never been certain.

But the choices were very few.

5

TO SHORE

Watchfulness is the law of the ship,—watch on watch,
for advantage and for life.
               —RALPH WALDO EMERSON, *ENGLISH TRAITS* (1856)

"A Carnival of Murder on the High Seas," announced the
Halifax Herald, the evening paper of the Canadian port
where the *Herbert Fuller* arrived on the morning of July 21, a week
after the killings. "One of the most thrilling tales of murder on
the high seas ever related in the new world, startles the people
of this continent today." This was not an overstatement. News of
the *Fuller* murders appeared in hundreds of American newspapers
in every state, from New York to Los Angeles, Maine to Texas,
and across Canada, most often under page 1 headlines. "For cold
blooded butchery," concluded the *Boston Globe*, "the crime has few
parellels [*sic*]." Versions of what had occurred aboard the ship and
how it managed to find its way to shore would emerge in bits and
pieces over the coming days.

The ship was met by a pilot outside the harbor at six in the morning and brought in to the anchorage. Trailing behind the ship was
one of its two small boats, in which the three bodies had been placed

the morning of their discovery. The dock was already crowded as the boat was brought alongside: "The stench was frightful and those nearest the water hastened away." Somebody official cut the fastenings of the boat's canvas cover and ripped it open, exposing the bodies: "They were wrapped in white shrouds, which were soaked with slime, salt water, blood and decaying matter." "It was a terrible sight," wrote another observer, "or rather, more horrible from what was not seen, but felt, than what was discernable. . . . There they were—lying beside each other, undistinguishable from bags of merchandise, in their horrible companionship of days!" The crowd on the dock "pushed and swayed" to catch a glimpse of the corpses, but they were seen by only a few officials and reporters "and were not exposed to satisfy the morbid curiosity of the crowd." The bodies were brought up and placed in wooden boxes. "The corpses presented a ghastly, sickening sight as the canvas was lifted from the silent forms. The faces were covered with dried clotted blood and their hair was disheveled and matted; the men were dressed in underclothing, which was torn and soaked with crimson fluid. The canvas was quickly dropped back; none cared to gaze for more than a few moments at the soul-rendering spectacle." The bodies were taken off to the city morgue; the crowd there was mostly women. "Many of them fainted and it was no more than they deserved."

The survivors, meanwhile, were all brought ashore and taken to the police station. All were under arrest, though their status varied. In the past week, suspicions among the survivors had settled first on Charley Brown and then on Tom Bram. Both arrived in Halifax as prisoners of the other seven; Brown had been chained at the base of the main mast, Bram at the mizzen. Now, the two suspects were placed in separate jail cells. Bram, though, was quickly reported to be the single "suspected murderer." The other crew members, including the steward, Spencer, were put together in other cells, while Lester Monks, officially under arrest, was confined only to the police chief's office, with an officer as guard. The deference shown Monks, well dressed and identified as a Harvard student, included the favor of sending a telegram.

"Ship at Halifax. Come at once." Frank Monks had no idea what his son's telegram on the morning of the twenty-first meant. He thought perhaps the ship had been wrecked or disabled in some way and Lester might be a victim. He rushed to the Boston Chamber of Commerce, where from various reports he learned the reason for the ship's arrival in Halifax and that Lester was uninjured. But barely two weeks after he had sent his worrisome son away for what he expected would be many months, if not more, Frank Monks once again found himself enmeshed in Lester's troubles. The senior Monks made plans to get to Halifax as fast as possible, by train, with his brother George to accompany him. Frank Monks also hired Frank G. Forbes, "a clever young Halifax barrister."

Lester—white, well spoken, and the only surviving native American of the *Fuller*'s people—quickly became the focus of newspaper attentions. His "is the only narrative, reliable or unreliable as it may be, that can be ascertained so far," hedged the *Washington Evening Times* late on the twenty-first. Morrill Goddard was less cautious. Goddard, the editor of the *New York Sunday Journal*, telegraphed Monks: "Will you write story of experiences on board the Fuller for Sunday Journal in about two thousand words and telegraph it tomorrow, Thursday evening? Will send you check for such article at usual magazine rates. Wire answer my expense." A handwritten "Please" was added before the last instruction. Monks did not reply.

Monks did make a statement, to a local reporter who happened to get a few minutes with him late on the twenty-first. It was the first public accounting of what happened on the *Herbert Fuller*.

At the time of the murder I occupied an apartment between the chart room and the captain's cabin. To the right of the cabin was the room occupied by the second mate. At the time of the murder the captain was in the chart room. We all retired about 11 o'clock on the night of the July 13. Toward 1 o'clock in the morning I was awakened by screams. I thought I might possibly have been dreaming, and lay over on my side. A few seconds after I heard another scream. I realized that the alarm came from Mrs. Nash. I grabbed my revolver, and took time only to put on my trousers, and ran out with the revolver in my hand to ascertain the cause.

I had to pass the captain's chart room. The light was burning, and I saw the captain dead on the floor. I heard footsteps in the companionway, and followed them to the deck. There I confronted the first mate. He had a billet of wood in his hand, and assumed a threatening attitude. I leveled my revolver at him, and asked him who had committed the murder.

The first mate said he did not know, and we decided to investigate. All hands were called up. The colored steward and I and the mate decided to put Charles Brown, who was at the wheel at the time [of the murders], in irons. In the morning I made the following report in the log book:

> *"On this day the steward of the said Herbert Fuller came to me and told me that the sailors all came and made an open statement to him in reference to one of the sailors whose name is Charles Brown. The statement was to his conduct of guilt in regard to the murder which took place on board said vessel. At once we got each man's statement. On the strength of these statements we concluded to put him in irons. At daybreak, at 7 a.m., all hands were mustered aft and thoroughly searched, and no other weapons were given them but their knives. Each man was then placed a certain distance apart from each other until after hours. Myself, the steward and the mate were stationed amidship, and a good lookout kept until daylight."*

Charles Brown, who was put in irons, made a subsequent statement accusing the mate of the murder. He said he saw him kill the captain through the transom over the chart room. The steering of the ship was then entrusted to the first mate.

The cook, who knew something of navigation, looked at the compass two days after the murder and said the first mate was not steering the course given him. He was steering the ship in an opposite direction. This looked suspicious, and the cook and myself after consultation decided to have the first mate placed under arrest. He was taken unawares and placed in irons. The cook then navigated the vessel to a point off Halifax harbor.

We tried to get the ship back to Boston, but owing to the wind at the time we were obliged to make for the Nova Scotia coast and brought up near Sable Island. We drifted about in the fog for some time and finally saw a pilot, who brought the Fuller into this port. We kept the bodies for three days, as long as we could. The odor of decomposition then became unbearable, and we decided to place them in a boat and cover them with canvass. The boat was towed behind the vessel.

The experience on board was enough to make the stoutest heart quail, and it was a great relief to my pent-up feelings when we came to anchor in Halifax.

This first account of what happened on the *Herbert Fuller* provided some answers to the mystery but created many more questions; many details would be proved wrong. Monks did not retire at eleven o'clock; he did not put on his trousers; there were no footsteps to hear in the cabin. Bram never steered the ship; Spencer knew nothing about navigation; Boston was never an option. And so forth. It is unclear how Monks quoted an extended logbook entry. Subsequent revelations would prove essential portions of Monks's account at best incomplete and at worst duplicitous. But if Monks's statement to the reporter was designed to focus suspicion on Bram, it was very effective.

Still, one logical question about Monks's actions, or lack of action, immediately occurred to reporters. "The passenger must have slumbered deeply or been strangely deaf to his surroundings not to have heard something of what was going on on the other side of the thin partitions," observed the *Washington Evening Times*. "The murders were not committed without noise for the fiendish killing was accomplished with an ax, and the victims were butchered in a most sickening manner." The *Halifax Herald* also wondered: "One of the most mysterious elements in this terrible crime is how [Bram], or whoever did the murder, could kill two men and almost finish a third [murder] without wakening Monks."

There is no definitive narrative of what happened on the *Herbert Fuller* from the time of the murders to the end of the abbreviated voyage eight days later in Halifax. Nine survivors, one of them the killer, each told his own tale, varying in length, detail, and reason. Most of the men just told what little they knew; some told what they imagined; at least one told what might prove rewarding—a salvage fee worth more than two years of regular wages; one told lies to cover his tracks as the killer.

The one version that the survivors at least nominally agreed to was written up by Monks during the morning after the murders, while the bodies were prepared and placed in the ship's boat. He wrote in pencil on four sheets of New York hotel stationery that Bram provided. Spelling and punctuation were imperfect, as might be expected in the sleepless hours after three murders.

TUESDAY, JULY 14, 1896.

Monday night everything on board of the barkentine "Herbert Fuller" was perfectly quite and peaceful. The crew had no fault to find with any thing on board. The second mate had the watch from 8 until 12. I went to bed about 8 o'clock, the steward says the Captain had been drinking but I did not notice it. I am naturally a very heavy sleeper so do not know so the murders which were committed might have happened before I woke up.

My first recollections are these: I heard a scream followed by a gurlling noise, as if someone was choking. I reached down and got a box of shells for my revolver and filled the pistol, which I kept under my pillow, as fast as possible. Then I called "Captain Nash"; as I got no answer I unlocked my cabin door and stepped out into the after-cabin. The Captain slepted on a cot placed against the starboard wall. The Captain was lying on the floor with the couch tipped up on end. I went up to him and shook him. I found he was covered with blood. I ran into Mrs. Nash's room to call her, I could see that sheets of her bunk were covered with blood. I then ran forward to the forward companion way and looked on the deck. I saw the mate Mr. Bram on deck. I called to him. I held my revolver pointed toward him, when he saw me, he picked up a board to throw at me, but I called out. "It's me Mr. Monks; come below for Gods sake" he came below and we took the lantern in the foreward cabin and went into the after-cabin. I slipped on a pair of trousers and a shirt, he grabbed his revolver, and we ran on deck. We did not know who were our friends or foes. We crouched down on the deck to windard just abreast of the mizzen mast. Mr. Bram covered the man at the wheel, and I kept my revolver pointed forwards. It was very dark. In this way we sat waiting for daylight. We then went forward and banged on the galley door for the steward. J. Spencer. He came on deck and we told him what had happened. He went aft and went into the cabin, while Bram and myself kept on deck with our revolvers. He came running out of the cabin in a few minutes and said the second mate Mr Blum was lying dead in his birth. [A pencil line leads from here to the top of the page where the following sentence is written: We found a bloody ax on the deck, which we threw overboard as we feared the crew would use it against us.] We then went aft in a body and questioned the man at the wheel, he said he did not know anything had happened, and had heard no unusual noises. We then went forward and woke up the crew. They all appeared greatly astonished and all protested they knew nothing. We all then went aft in a body and went into the cabin. The second mate was lying dead in his bunk. Mrs. Nash was lying in her bunk with her clothes pulled up. Captain Nash was lying on the floor dead. We went on deck and at once decided to steer for French Cayane, that being the nearest port.

My theory of the tragedy is this:

The second mate Mr Blum, had been drinking, and went below and tried to rape Mrs. Nash, Captain Nash woke up and went and got an ax (the one we threw overboard) and attempted to kill Blum and his wife. Blum must off gotten the ax and hit the captain and then staggered on deck and then back to his bunk.

Lester Hawthorne Monks.

Under Monks's signature appeared this addendum:

The second mate offered Mr Bram a drink at about 12 o'clock. This whiskey made Mr. Bram very sick while on deck with me, and he acted as if he had been drugged.

Lester Hawthorne Monks.
Thomas M. Bram Mate
Jonathan Spencer
Charles Brown
Frank Loheac
Folke Wassin
[and added on the back]
Henry J. Slice Oscar Andersson Hendrik Perdok

Much would be made of this extraordinary document in the months ahead, in particular whether Monks was the creator of it or, as he would insist, merely the transcriber of Bram's narration. The idea that the crime was a closed circle of victims and perpetrators would be openly ridiculed. Still, the detail of Monks's actions before Bram's involvement must be Monks's own creation, and there is much odd about it. Monks wrote that the murders "*might* have happened before I woke up." But the murders *must* have happened before Monks woke up, *unless* of course he was up all along and involved with them. Whether Monks was a "heavy sleeper" is unproven; the account of his youthful sailing adventure six years earlier suggests that he wasn't. Whether he "shook" Nash and found him "covered with blood" were assertions Monks would later deny.

Monks's strange statement elided much detail. Following is a fuller version of events, assembled from accounts given in newspapers, courtrooms, and elsewhere:

After Monks says he saw blood on Laura Nash's bed, he "suddenly realized that the scream I heard meant something." It is a dramatic line, though it is notable that no one other than Monks heard the scream, if in fact there was a scream. In any case, he decided it would be safer on deck than to remain in the cabin. Still in his pajamas, Monks first moved through the cabin toward the after companionway but had not gotten very far before considering that someone could be waiting above the companionway to attack him. Monks did not specifically say so, but for this to have happened, within several feet of the helmsman—Loheac at the time—would have meant that a mutiny was under way and Loheac was at least aware of it, if not voluntarily involved. Monks reversed course and made his way to the bottom on the forward companionway, passing the first mate's cabin to his left and the second mate's cabin to his right. Monks had now passed through the entire length of the cabin without encountering any threats. Looking up, he saw Bram walking the deck, "up and down . . . between the mainmast and the mizzenmast, from the starboard side to the port side." Bram's crossings from port to starboard were on a line roughly twenty feet forward of the companionway. This was the first mate's normal position when on watch.

What the time was is unspecified, other than being sometime after two o'clock, because Loheac was the helmsman. He had been called to the helm by Bram. "I was close to the mainmast and so was Bram, on the starboard side," Loheac later recalled. "Bram said to me 'Four bells.'" It appears that bells were not rung, but this was not unusual, especially given that the relief helmsman and the mate, who called the changes, were near each other.

How long Monks, at the base of the companionway, observed Bram is unclear. Monks said later, "I don't think it could have been more than 10 minutes" from when he heard Laura Nash's supposed scream to when he took up his position at the bottom of the forward companionway. It may have been that, or less, or more. There is what Monks said; there is no one to confirm or refute it. He was, at that point, the only person alive in the cabin. If it was a total of ten minutes, it is possible that Monks had reached the companionway no more than five minutes after the scream. This gave Monks ample time to observe Bram's movements. Again, because Monks was the only person who claimed to have heard a scream—not Bram forward or Brown aft—it is possible that Monks had even more time after her murder to decide what to do.

"Mr. Bram!" Monks finally called. His revolver was pointed at Bram and visible. Startled, Bram picked up a loose board. What happened next depends on whose version is the truth. At this point, the number of active, surviving participants in the drama doubles from one to two.

According to Monks, Bram "picked up a plank and threw it towards me," but "instead of going in the hatchway, it went across— it did not come in." Monks then identified himself to Bram and said, in something like a stage whisper, "Come below. The captain has been murdered." It is odd that Monks referred only to the captain, knowing that his wife was also dead. Bram replied, "No, no, no." And Monks, with peculiar toploftiness, said, "Come below and see for yourself." Assured that Monks meant him no harm, Bram descended.

According to Bram, on the other hand, "I saw someone standing in the forward companionway of the after cabin with a revolver pointing at me. . . . I didn't hesitate; I picked up a piece of board that was standing here by the mainsheet and held the board in front of me." Monks then did call out to Bram, not calling Bram's name, as Monks said, but merely, "Who is that?" To which Bram replied, "It is me." Then Monks called out, "Come down here," to which Bram replied, "What is wrong?" And Monks's reply, according to Bram: "Come down here, Mr. Bram, don't be afraid, it is me; the captain is killed."

Bram's reply to that information was not a curious trio of "No's" but only a disbelieving "What!" Only then did Bram relinquish the board: "Thinking that I was far enough away from the companionway, I let the board drop, and it slid right down the steps and went down to the bottom of the stairway." After Bram joined Monks in the cabin, "I threwed this piece of board back on deck." Regardless of whose version was true, from this point in the dark and bloodied cabin of the *Herbert Fuller* and for many decades after, the fortunes of Lester Monks and Thomas Bram would be twisted together.

Whatever happened in their tense confrontation moments before, Monks and Bram were now in the cabin at the bottom of the companionway, between Bram's room and the second mate's room. Bram suggested he get from his room an old revolver he had; Monks agreed and waited. If he feared Bram, this would have been the time to take action to prevent Bram from arming himself. Instead, Monks waited outside. Presently, Bram appeared, with his revolver, and Monks and Bram proceeded through the cabin toward the chart room. On the way, Bram took the lantern hanging over the dining table and turned it up bright.

According to Monks, they went through the chart room and into Monks's cabin without stopping to check on the captain, who was still making sounds. Bram "didn't go up and examine . . . Capt. Nash at all," said Monks; he "passed right into my room." Bram waited outside Monks's room while he changed from his pajamas to duck trousers and a flannel shirt. The lantern, on full blaze, was placed, apparently by Monks, on the floor near the entrance to his room.

At one point, according to Monks, Bram began to move away, but Monks ordered him back. When Monks was done changing, the two men moved quickly through the cabin and up the forward companionway, not stopping at Laura Nash's room and for some reason leaving the lantern behind, on the cabin floor.

Bram told a mostly similar account, except for two important details. Entering the chart room, Bram observed that "sure enough, the captain laid there dead, or very near dead. Once in a while there would be a kind of a gurgling. Quite a while afterwards there would be another one." Noting this, "I went over to his feet and felt of his feet and his feet was cold. With that I ran back into Monks' room and stationed myself by the door."

Bram explained, correctly, that by feeling an injured person's feet, one could ascertain if blood is still flowing in the body; the captain's feet were cold, meaning blood was no longer flowing and he was dead.

When Monks had dressed, Bram said, "Let us go into Mrs. Nash's room and see Mrs. Nash's room." This was a reasonable suggestion that Bram says Monks rejected: "It ain't no use going there; I have been there; she is dead already."

It is perhaps understandable that when he had been alone in the cabin a few minutes earlier, Monks decided that seeing Laura's bloodstained sheets was enough. It is incomprehensible that after spending time in the cabin with Bram that Monks would not take the opportunity to confirm his assumption, or perhaps find her still alive and needing attention. It is inexplicable that Monks insisted that Bram and he not investigate whether in fact "she is dead already." Monks would have no certainty of knowing if she was dead . . . unless of course he somehow did.

The passenger and the mate gained the deck without incident and sat down along the starboard railing near the mizzenmast, pondering what to do next. After a few moments, according to Bram, Monks asked, "Where is the second mate?" Bram answered, "It is his watch below; ain't he in his room?" "I didn't see him," said Monks, though it is unclear when or whether Monks tried to find him. "Well," said Bram, "if he is not down there, he is forward with the men."

Monks gave a slightly different story: "Where is the second mate?" he asked Bram. "I am going to wake him." Monks got up and made moves to get Blomberg, which prompted Bram to say, "There is a mutiny. The second mate is forward with the crew." According to Monks, Bram said if he and Monks went forward, the crew "might probably rush us."

For whatever reason—a possible mutiny or simply an absent second mate who might have had something to do with the killings in the aft cabin—Monks and Bram decided to stay put until daylight when they would wake the steward. In the meantime, they decided to take up defensive positions on the cabin top.

First, though, Bram had something of a breakdown. He began to cry, went down to his knees, and grasped Monks's knees, begging him for protection from a crew that wanted to kill him for his arguably harsh treatment of them, particularly Brown and Blomberg. Monks, without much sympathy, said he'd do what he could.

That was not enough to settle Bram's nerves. He started to feel sick and, Monks later said, put a finger in his throat and vomited. The nausea was prompted, said Bram, according to Monks, by some whiskey Blomberg had given him at the midnight watch change. Bram said the whiskey had been drugged and that Blomberg had said he got the alcohol from Monks. After giving Bram the drink from a small tin cup, Blomberg had thrown it overboard, according to Bram.

After Bram vomited, Monks told him to get up and walk around. "He sort of staggered round the deck," said Monks, "and then sat down again." Bram, for his part, later said, "Absolutely not," that he had staggered. The vomit, a small amount, remained there for the time being.

Monks and Bram took seated positions next to each other on the forward end of the cabin top, Bram facing aft with his revolver pointed in the direction of the helmsman, Monks facing forward, his weapon pointed at whoever might appear from the darkness. If either was inclined to silence the other, this was a fine opportunity; neither took it. Two hours passed and nothing happened. At four, with light on the eastern horizon, Monks and Bram went forward to wake Spencer. Neither showed any concern about running into Blomberg, who supposedly had gone forward to mutiny with the crew.

Normally, four o'clock would have been time for the watch change, but the second mate was unaccounted for and there was no sign of his watchmates appearing from the forward cabin. Loheac, on the wheel for the second two hours of his four-hour watch, made no move to give up the helm, even though he knew, if not by a clock then by dawn's approach at least, that the time for the next watch had come. In the gathering light, he had discerned Monks and Bram and their weapons and chose to stay at his position and see what developed.

Bram knocked on the galley door. After a moment, Spencer appeared, bare chested in long underwear, and made a good-morning salute. He did not seem at all questioning of why the mate and the passenger, armed with pistols, had woken him, though it was extraordinary in the least for the passenger to be in the forward cabin.

Monks did not waste time. "The captain has been murdered," he said.

"Oh, I guess not," said Spencer, not yet grasping the situation.

"Well," said Monks, giving an encore performance of his earlier words to Bram, "go look for yourself."

Spencer dressed and led the three men toward the aft cabin top. On the way, he asked Bram where the second mate was; as he earlier told Monks, Bram said Blomberg must be forward with crew. Earlier, this might have been possible, but now that Bram and Monks had gone forward to get Spencer and shown no concern for Blomberg's whereabouts, it was a strange thing for Bram to say and for Monks and Spencer to leave unchallenged.

Spencer went up on the cabin top and looked through the skylight; he saw the captain lying on the floor of the chart room. Spencer came off the roof and started to go below to investigate further, but Monks stopped him. "I wouldn't go down in that cabin without a revolver," Monks warned the steward. Spencer asked Bram to lend him his, and Bram did; Bram then asked Monks to lend him his revolver, and Monks refused.

Not trusting Bram's revolver, Spencer went to the railing and pulled the trigger. Nothing. "I pulled three or four times on the trigger and at last it went off." Apparently, no one else on the ship heard the gun fire, suggesting that the various noises made by a ship under sail—sails, rigging, hull, water—were loud enough to muffle the sound of a gunshot on deck, to say nothing of a woman's scream from a cabin.

Spencer opened the cylinder and discovered all of the cartridges were nicked, indicating that the hammer had struck them previously and failed to fire them. Bram explained that the gun was old and that he had never actually fired it himself. Spencer gave the gun back to Bram and, unarmed, went below.

Without apparent fear or concern for his own welfare, Spencer moved through the cabin to the chart room. There he saw the captain dead and, without going to him, headed back toward the forward companionway. Approaching it, "my eyes dropped on the second mate," dead in his bed. Spencer rushed back to the deck.

"Jesus Christ!" he yelled at Bram. "What is this?"

According to Spencer, neither Bram nor Monks reacted. "Nothing, nobody said nothing, nothing was said."

According to Monks, he turned around to Bram and said, "I thought you said the second mate was forward," to which Bram replied, "Well, he was forward."

Then came another surprise: the discovery of the murder weapon.

According to Spencer, Bram looked across to the port side of the ship and said to him, "That is the axe."

According to Monks, Bram said, "There is an axe. . . . There is the axe that did it." According to Bram, however, "I did not find the axe. The steward saw it first." It was Spencer who said, "There is an axe," pointing to where Monks and Bram then saw it. According to Bram, the axe was directly to port of the forward end of the after house, "on a line with the forward part of the after house," that is, fairly close for whoever had brought it up the companionway.

All agreed that it was Spencer who walked from where the three of them were standing on the starboard side over to the port side and grabbed the axe from where it was stuck under a lashing plank securing the deck load of lumber, blade in, handle out. "I pulled the axe up there and I looked at the axe, bringing it up to windward," Spencer later said. "There was blood on the axe and the steel was bright, and two hand marks on the handle."

After Spencer inspected it, he passed the axe to Bram, who said to him and Monks, "What will we do with it?" According to Bram, Monks answered, "For God's sake throw it overboard or else the crew will use it on us," and Spencer agreed. "Yes, throw it overboard." And Bram did.

Monks remembered similarly. "The mate he held onto the axe, he pulled on the axe, and pulled on it again and I let it go."

According to Spencer, Bram cried, "This is the axe that done it, this is the axe that done it. . . . Must I throw it overboard?" Spencer said no, but Monks said yes, and Bram with another cry threw it into the Atlantic.

"You should not do that," said Spencer, to which Bram said, "But we don't find no axe."

"What do you take me for, a God damn fool?" said Spencer. "Don't you know a man had seen you with the axe?"—meaning Loheac at the wheel.

Indeed, Loheac claimed to have witnessed the entire discussion. "I saw Jonathan Spencer stoop down and bring up an axe," Loheac later said. "Next, I saw that Bram had it in his hands, I heard Bram giving a yell, and next I saw the axe fall into the water."

Moments later, Spencer, Monks, and Bram came aft to question Loheac directly, but not about the axe. "Jonathan Spencer pointed a revolver," said Loheac, "and asked me if I hear any noise, and I answered 'no.'"

Loheac would also claim that two hours earlier, shortly after he had come to the wheel, he had seen Bram "appear in the forward companionway, running for the deck. . . . Hardly had the mate got on the deck load when I heard the passenger Monks call to him 'Mr. Bram.'" This squares with Monks's first account but not with his second version, in which he said he watched Bram walking the deck, for several minutes or more, before he called out to Bram.

Monks, Spencer, and Bram moved forward to the middle of the ship and decided that their next move was to wake the crew. First, though, there was the matter of Bram's vomit. They found themselves standing close by the small pool of it.

According to Spencer, Bram repeated to him what he earlier told Monks, that he had gotten a drink of drugged whiskey from Blomberg, who, according to Bram, said he had gotten it from Monks. Spencer "went up and looked at it" and noted "it smelt strong of liquor." According to Spencer, Bram said, "Shall we take it ashore and have it analyzed?" and Spencer said yes. But then Bram, who had been perched on the railing, somehow "fell down into the spew."

According to Monks, "Mr. Bram sat down on it. . . . He was sort of sitting up against the rail and he sat right down, slid right along, wiped it up."

"Jesus Christ," said Spencer, "you haven't got anything there to take up now," as Bram rubbed it in the seat of his pants "and made me a foolish answer."

For his part, Bram said, "I got sick to my stomach from seeing the sight down below, and throwed up a very little on the weather side."

It was Monks, said Bram, who suggested that "you probably might have been drugged," to which Bram replied, "I don't think the second mate had any drug in that bottle; what do you know about it?"

"Well," said Monks, not answering the question, "you don't know what was in that liquor."

"That didn't make me sick," said Bram, "I don't believe, because there is very little of it throwed up."

It was not the bit of whiskey Bram got from Blomberg but the gruesome murder of the captain—the only victim Bram had yet seen—that turned his stomach. "I never mentioned a word about [being] drugged . . . to Mr. Monks. . . . Mr. Monks presented that."

As to his slipping into the vomit, Bram said, "My feet slipped someway or other from under me, and . . . the slippers that I had on got into this little bit of stuff, this bread sandwich. We stood on the deck there then, and there was nothing . . . said about analyzation."

As to Monks's assertion that Bram had earlier brought the vomit up with a finger in throat, Bram said, "I am positive I did not. . . . [I]t came up of its own free will and accord."

What was the importance of Bram's vomit and his wiping it up, intentionally or not, before a sample could be saved? If he was the murderer, his actions suggested an attempt to destroy evidence that might somehow point to his guilt. If he was not the murderer, perhaps someone *had* poisoned the alcohol. Or perhaps Bram, as he said, had simply been sickened by the sight of the dead captain, vomited a small amount, and then had accidently slipped in it. In either case, it was Spencer who was worked up about it. Monks simply noted it. The discussion ended, as greater matters were at hand.

It was time to gather the crew. Brown, on watch forward, was sent below to get Anderson, Slice, and Wassen; apparently, they were still asleep below, now some amount of time since their watch was supposed to have started at four.

The five crewmen, including Brown's watchmate Perdok, assembled on the middeck. They were told of the murders—it is unclear by whom precisely—and sent into the aft cabin to view the bodies, accompanied by Spencer and Bram. Monks couldn't go. "I got as far as the second mate's door and turned around and came back," he said. "I saw the second mate in there all cut up." Of course, a few hours earlier he supposedly had been face-to-face with the similarly butchered captain.

Back on deck, Spencer raised a new issue. "The captain's revolver is missing," he said to Bram, "and the murderer has got it." The crew were all searched; no revolver was found. The need to find the captain's revolver became acute. Monks piped up. "Will you go down with me," he asked Spencer, "and look in the bed space [of my cabin]?" Spencer said yes. Taking Wassen with them, the three went below. They went first to Mrs. Nash's room because, said Spencer, that is where the captain's revolver was usually kept. "I seen it there," said Spencer, "about a week before," in a drawer. The gun wasn't there. They went to Monks's room. Entering first, Wassen "got hold of the bed [and] he pulled the revolver out." It had been between the bunk's two thin mattresses, at the head of the berth. The revolver was loaded. Wassen handed it to Monks, Spencer said, "Give it to me," and Monks did so.

No one asked then or later how the weapon got from one cabin to the other, or why Monks had suggested the search of his own room, or how long the loaded weapon had been under Monks's head. "I had never seen it before," Monks asserted later, though it is hard to understand how he never felt the lump of a gun beneath his mattress, supposedly during his ten nights of sleeping on it. It is also hard to understand how Laura Nash, who made up Monks's bed, had not come across the revolver for a week, if indeed the gun had been there the whole time.

In any case, Monks told Spencer to tell Wassen, "Don't tell the rest of them" that the revolver had been found. Spencer dutifully said to Wassen, "Don't tell the rest of them you found it." Wassen promptly went back on deck and forward and, for whatever reason, told everyone. Monks's reaction is unknown; Spencer, apparently thinking to intimidate the crew, showed the revolver to them.

Next came a cursory investigation about whether anyone knew anything about the killings. Bram led the questioning.

"Brown do you know anything about this murder?"

Brown said, "I know nothing about it, sir."

"Have you heard any unusual noise while you were at the wheel?"

Brown said, "I heard nothing, I don't know nothing about it."

Bram asked the same questions of Loheac, Slice, Perdok, Wassen, and Anderson; all said they knew nothing.

Spencer likewise: "I am sure I know nothing about it, for I was sleeping forward." Monks said, "I didn't know anything about it until I heard Mrs. Nash's scream."

"As far as I am concerned," said Bram, "I know nothing about it myself."

Only one conclusion was possible. "Well," said Bram, "if that is the case, I can't blame anybody for this occurrence. . . . The people are dead and they cannot answer for themselves, and God only knows how it occurred."

Others agreed that Bram put the conclusion slightly differently: according to Monks, Bram said, "We mustn't blame the living for the dead; the dead cannot speak for themselves." Anderson and Loheac concurred with Monks's version.

From this came the scenario recorded in Monks's written statement that morning: the second mate had attempted to rape the captain's wife; the captain intervened and killed her and mortally wounded the second mate; the second mate had killed him, stashed the axe on deck, and died in his bunk.

Fantastic as that might be, there remained the practical question of what to do with the bodies. According to Bram, he said, "What are we going to do with these people? They can't stay down there; it will be offensive in a few days and then we will have to throw them overboard."

Slice said, "I think it would be a good idea to put those bodies in the small boat and put canvas on it." Bram considered the idea "a good one, we all agreed to it and with that I ordered this boat to be brought on deck."

Monks, however, claimed that Bram simply suggested throwing the bodies overboard and cleaning up the blood in the cabin and that Spencer countered with, "No, we will leave them just where they are."

Monks and others agreed that it was Slice's suggestions that were adopted. "We doesn't throw the bodies overboard," said Slice. "We must take them in as evidence, and we doesn't clean the cabin out, either; we must leave it just as it is." He added that by taking the bodies as evidence, they would be saved "for the family at the same time."

At about this time—specifically when is unclear—Monks discovered a trail of blood between the forward companionway and the place where the axe was found. Daylight had long come;

Monks, Bram, and Spencer had been in the vicinity for an hour or more; and the crew had all been in and out of the aft cabin, passing close by the blood trail, but nobody had noticed it until now. It was "a sort of dripping of blood all along on the house," as Monks later described it. "It started on the deck load and went aft across the after house."

Actually, he later clarified, the apparent creation of the trail was in the opposite direction: the trail started at the forward companionway, went up and back on the after house where there was some pooling, and then went forward in increasingly smaller drops to where the axe was found under the stringer. The trail left little doubt as to how it was created: the murderer had exited the cabin with the bloody axe via the forward companionway, had first placed the axe on top of the after house, and then, after a period during which some blood had pooled, had taken the axe just forward of the cabin and stuck the blade into the deck load.

Now it was time to prepare the bodies for their interment in the ship's smaller boat. The jolly boat, as it was called—the origin of the term is unknown—was taken from its place upside down on top of the forward cabin and lashed right side up on the deck load forward of the main mast. Brown was sent below to get a sewing kit, which happened to be in Blomberg's room. Brown had to climb over the body to retrieve the kit, getting Blomberg's blood on his clothes in the process. Brown later made sure to point out to the others how his clothes happened to get bloody. Spare canvas and sheets were brought from the forward cabin.

All six crewmen were needed to get the heavy bodies on deck; it was a gruesome task. Towels were placed over the faces and heads. Brown stitched material around Mrs. Nash before her exposed body was brought on deck; the men were brought up as they were and shrouded on deck. The captain's body was placed first in the jolly boat, in the center. His wife was placed to his left—closest to his heart—and Blomberg placed to his right.

While the crew was engaged with the bodies, Monks steered the ship, briefly. It turned out that a good small boat sailor was not necessarily a ship's helmsman. In the moderate breeze, Monks couldn't keep the ship from turning up into the wind; Slice rushed back to take the wheel. Relieved of sailing duty, Monks was given another by Bram. "We will have to make some report of this, some account of it," Bram said to Monks. "It is best for you to write out your theory." And so, Monks, on writing paper from a New York hotel provided by Bram, "started with a lead pencil to write his theory."

When the bodies were in the boat, Brown asked Bram if it should be covered. "No, hold on Charley," said Monks before Bram answered, "We might do some praying." There were no objections. The survivors gathered around for an impromptu funeral service.

Bram, a veteran of prayer meetings in Dennett restaurants, suggested that the small organ in the chart room be brought up, "and I will play a hymn." According to Bram, "We had some trouble getting the organ up and I told the men not to bother about it." According to Monks, he said, "No, that is foolishness," before any attempt was made. Monks then read, from an Episcopal Book of Common Prayer that he somehow had in his possession, the service for the burial of the dead at sea. "Unto Almighty God we commend the soul of our brother departed," it starts, "and we commit his body to the deep." No one noted that the brutalized bodies were not in fact being buried at sea but had been crudely embalmed and were to be kept in a boat on deck. When Monks was done, canvas was spread over the boat and carefully tacked down, with just an inch between tacks.

When that work was done, Monks read to the group the statement he had prepared and already signed, with the additional theorizing at the bottom. Bram signed. "I believed it all at the time it was drawn up. I knew nothing to the contrary then." Everyone else signed as well, whether they believed it or not. Spencer, for one, did not. "That ain't so there; them people didn't kill theirself, nothing of the kind," he said when the document was presented to him. Later he explained: "I signed it because I didn't want them to know that I knew as much as I did; didn't want to be too smart; signed it more for peace than anything else. I didn't want them to think that I doubted what they say."

That Spencer considered every other survivor one of "them" and not one of "us" reflects the general attitude aboard the ship. No one knew who was the killer, but each knew it was one of them. For the remainder of their time at sea, everyone slept on deck; no one spent any significant time below. After the bodies were brought up, the aft cabin was padlocked, the handles of tools kept in the forward cabin carpenter shop were cut off, and the shop door was nailed shut.

With Nash dead, Bram became the senior officer. By law of the sea, he was in charge, but by behavior he was wavering, seeking consensus on decisions rather than exerting his authority. He appointed Brown first mate and Loheac second mate. Each was nominally in charge of their respective watches of three men apiece; in practice, everyone would be on deck at all times. There was no off watch per se; everyone stayed on deck, and none slept much or soundly, eight wary of becoming the next victim, one careful not to reveal himself.

Now came the business of getting the ship to port. "We have got to make the nearest port possible," said Monks. He asked Bram what that port was, and Bram said, "French Kyan." That is, Cayenne, in French Guiana, just north of Brazil.

If not taking up the role of captain with gusto, Bram was the only practical navigator on board. No one else knew where they were or what course to steer for another place. Bram said, correctly, that it would be easy downwind sailing to Cayenne and in the general direction of where the cargo was supposed to go.

It was also fifteen hundred miles away and, even if the favorable trade winds held, at least a week's sailing. Within three hours of taking a course to Cayenne, questions arose about the distance and the legal uncertainties of arriving in a remote foreign port with three murdered bodies.

The closest port was Bermuda, only four hundred miles to the west but directly into headwinds and thus perhaps longer to reach than Cayenne. Quickest to something like home was Halifax, seven hundred northerly miles with a favorable wind direction and proper police and port authorities.

As captain, it was Bram's choice; without argument, he acceded to popular wishes, and the ship was turned toward Halifax around noon on Tuesday, the fourteenth. From then on, two men were at the wheel at all times, by their own choosing. "They were very superstitious," said Monks, but it was not an unwise policy.

The rest of Tuesday passed without major incident. At some point, Brown threw his bloody clothes overboard, but it was understood by all that these were clothes soiled in his work on the bodies.

At some other point, Spencer said to Monks, "The mate killed them people." At least, that's what Spencer later claimed. Monks never confirmed or denied it.

Tuesday night everyone slept on deck, as they would for their remaining days at sea. By Wednesday at noon, by Bram's reckoning, they were just under six hundred miles from Halifax and proceeding quickly in moderate winds. Bram recorded the main event of the next eighteen hours in the ship's log, in his unschooled English:

On this day [Wednesday, the fifteenth], at 5.30 P.M., the steward of said H Fuller came to me and told me that the sailors all came and made an open statement to him in reference to one of the sailors whose name is Charles Brown's conduct of guilt in regard to the murder which took place on board said vessil. I at once got each mens statement Then upon the strength of these statements we concluded to put him in irons at daybreak at 7 PM all hands was musterd aft and throughly searcht and no other wepon was given them but their knives each man was then placed acertin distance apart from each other untop of the after house. Myself the steward & passenger was stationed amid ships well armed and kept a good lookout untill day break At 5 A M [on Thursday] Charles Brown was mancled and put in irons His actions all night was very suspicious and got himself all ready as it were to jump over the side but he was well garded by all hands on bord at 130 A M he mad an ~~desperate~~ effort [to] rush for the forward part of the ship but was instantly stop by the steward upon a pointed revolver towards him.

The log entry was signed by everyone except Perdok (who was at the wheel). The word *desperate* was crossed out at the insistence of Monks, who judged Brown's movement forward as not suspicious, and replaced, incongruously, by *effort*.

Brown's "conduct of guilt" was in his changed behavior starting the night of the murders, as noted by various crewmen. On his off watch before the murders, he had complained of "lots of insects in the forecastle" and brought his mattress and blankets up to sleep below the larger of the two boats on top of the cabin. During Tuesday, he had behaved strangely, avoiding other crewmen. On Tuesday night, he had gone up to Perdok and Anderson while they were sleeping "and peeped in our faces, and tell us to go to sleep." Bram heard from Loheac that Brown had been "telling me how easy it would be for a man to set the vessel afire." There was a barrel of kerosene in the forepeak, and "it wouldn't take long to spill it over the cargo and lit a match to it." On another occasion, Brown had been seen stripped to his pants and peering over the side of the ship, as if considering throwing himself overboard.

Wednesday evening, after Spencer had spoken to several sailors, he told Bram, "I have heard enough from those sailors to make me believe that that man killed those people." Bram said, "Very well," and with Spencer watching Bram wrote out the beginnings of his log entry.

At five in the morning on Thursday, Spencer, Bram, and Monks went forward to Brown, asleep on top of the forward cabin with his oilskin coat over his head, and Spencer, "swearing and cursing, calling me all the names he can find out," grabbed him. "Steward, you do wrong," Brown protested but did not resist. "You have killed those people," said Spencer. Brown was shackled to the base of the mizzenmast.

Though some on the *Herbert Fuller* then and others afterward, up to the present day, believe Brown was the killer, he could not have been. Surely, he was a strange duck who had had a mad spell several years earlier in which he shot at a man and would have a mad spell later in which he stabbed his nurse and would live out his days in an asylum, but for him to have been the *Fuller* killer was impossible. The simple fact is that he had no idea that there was an axe or where it was. Like every member of the regular crew, he was never in the aft cabin before the murders. He didn't know its layout, and he didn't know who slept where. Though he might have borne some animosity toward Bram, he had none toward the Nashes. If he had a mad spell, all the more unlikely that he could think to secure the wheel, grope his way through the darkened cabin, find the axe, kill three people and not disturb a fourth, and make his way back to the wheel before the ship went noticeably off course or Bram, pacing the deck, noticed him missing from the wheel.

Bram, though, with Brown chained, was satisfied that the mystery was solved. Bram went to him shortly after he was seized. Brown, shaking, asked Bram, "Did the passenger tell you he saw me kill those people?" Bram replied, "The passenger said nothing to me, but your actions to everybody denotes it."

According to Monks, Bram then came to him. "Now we have got the murderer," Bram supposedly told Monks, "we had better tear the paper you wrote up."

"We don't know that we have got the murderer," Monks supposedly said. "We won't tear it up; we will keep it."

Monks is the only source for this conversation. When asked about it later, Bram said the conversation never happened.

The next few days passed peaceably enough. The days were warm, the nights cool, and all adjusted to life on deck. Steady progress was made toward shore. At noon the day Brown was seized, Bram reckoned they had 460 miles to Halifax. According to his diligent log entries, the winds that day were light and variable, with a heavy sea and rain. Then the breeze came on strong from the west, and by noon Friday they had made over 260 northward miles, probably as much as the *Fuller* could make in a day. "All hands keeping a good lookout," Bram recorded.

What Bram knew to watch for was Sable Island, long and low in open ocean to the south of Nova Scotia, the so-called graveyard of the Atlantic. Soon the breeze dropped. By noon Saturday, they had made only 100 more miles but had safely passed to the west of Sable Island overnight; at eight in the morning, they were 30 miles beyond it. But the wind had disappeared.

As the ship drifted Saturday morning, the rudimentary nature of the burial given to the three murder victims became apparent: the bodies, rotting quickly in the summer air, stank. It was decided to lower the burial boat and tow it astern.

Soon afterward, Bram sighted a ship, a British steamer, about six miles off by Bram's estimate. Monks and Spencer had not seen it.

According to Bram, Spencer said, "It isn't no use signalizing that fellow."

Bram agreed: "We don't want to signalize him. We are all right. We have got good bearings on this island [Sable] for Halifax and we can go there all right—got our position all right now."

Monks said, "We had better signalize her, anyway, to tell her what happened to us." Bram, seeking consensus as usual, asked Spencer, "Will we do it?"

Spencer said, "Yes, it won't do no harm."

The ship's ensign, the American flag, was lowered and reraised upside down, a standard sign of distress.

Monks recalled differently.

He said, "We will signal her."

"Why?" asked Bram, "If we signal her what good will it do us?"

Monks said, "Well, we can get a navigator on board here."

Bram was insulted: "Don't you think I am a good enough navigator?"

Monks said, "No."

"Well," Bram supposedly said, "if we signal it will take all the glory away from us."

Monks replied that he "didn't care anything about glory, I wanted to get ashore."

Spencer, later, simply said the steamer was spotted, and he asked, "Shall we signalize her?" and Monks said, "Yes."

In addition to the upside-down ensign, a hand-cranked fog-horn was sounded continuously by crewmen, signal flags indicating "Mutiny; want assistance" were raised, and for good measure Spencer climbed the mizzen rigging and waved a white sheet. The steamer, after stopping to observe, soon continued on its way, likely confused by the various and conflicting actions.

Had the steamer approached the becalmed *Herbert Fuller*, and its precise situation then become known and communicated to maritime authorities, the voyage would have ended with Charley Brown the only person restrained and presumed guilty. This is not what happened.

What did happen depends on whose account to believe. Bram and Spencer gave similar accounts, saying that on Saturday just after the steamer motored away, Spencer grabbed Bram and he was ironed, just as Brown had been three days earlier.

"The mate was standing down [from] signalizing the steamboat," said Spencer, "and I brought him backwards and put my hand on him." Bram had been seated on the aft cabin top, and Spencer "brought him backwards . . . by his two shoulders, and I slipped my hands on him around there."

"What is this for?" asked Bram.

"For killing the Captain," said Spencer.

"I am innocent, steward," said Bram, whose face, according to Spencer, "turned red." Spencer pressed his revolver to Bram's face, prompting Bram to say, "Don't ill-treat a man, I am innocent." Nevertheless, Bram was ironed and "put on the mainmast."

Bram put it this way: "I walked aft . . . with the spyglass . . . looking at this steamer . . . and the next thing I knew the steward got me by the back of my throat . . . and throwed me down backwards." "What is this for?" Bram asked. All the sailors and Monks were there, and the steward held the revolver up to Bram's nose while holding him down. The mate made no resistance, and asked again, "What is this for?"

Spencer said, "For these people that are killed."

"Steward, I am an innocent man," Bram insisted. "I know nothing about this case." With that, Loheac brought a pair of irons, and Bram was bound.

Later, when Spencer brought him dinner, Bram pleaded again: "Steward, I am an entirely innocent man. I know nothing about this crime."

This time, Spencer acknowledged, "I don't believe that you killed those people, but you ought to know something about it. Being on deck you ought to have heard something." After Bram ate, Monks brought him a cigar: "I said the same thing to Mr. Monks [who] replied the same as the steward did to me."

This, according to Bram and Spencer, was all on Saturday. Seemingly inexplicably, Monks would say the holding of Bram happened on Sunday around noon, roughly twenty-four hours later. Anderson had come to Monks, saying Brown had told of seeing Bram in the chart room striking the captain once with an axe. For days, Brown had been afraid to say anything, but once he was ironed, he got up the nerve. "I like to be in irons," Brown by way of explanation said later, "till they find the right man that done it."

Spencer, for his part, did not confirm Brown's account.

Regardless of who was lying or telling the truth about how Bram came to be ironed, an explanation for holding Bram, beyond his possible responsibility for the murders, arose on Monday morning. It was raining, and Bram was taken down into the galley, where he continued with the ship's navigating. According to Bram, Spencer came to him and said, "Mr. Bram, if you had taken this vessel into port, you would get nothing for it, but by we taking her in they ought to give us at least $500 apiece for our trouble." Here was something like a motive for holding Bram that had nothing to do with his supposed involvement with the murders.

Unnamed members of the crew had told Spencer that $500 was a likely salvage fee for each of them. Spencer, suddenly not so plainly heroic as others would later say, would later admit that he had in mind a large reward for himself as "the sole person that brought the vessel ashore." At the very least, Spencer thought, "the Captain's folks ought to pay us something for bringing these bodies into port."

For Bram to bring the ship in would be merely his duty; neither crew nor Spencer would be entitled to anything but their pay. For Spencer, with the crew's assistance, to bring in the ship would arguably mean rewards for him and them. And so, with Halifax nearly in sight, Bram was seized. At least, that is one explanation for it.

The fog had cleared Sunday afternoon; that night, a lighthouse on an island fifty miles east of Halifax was sighted. Monday at noon, the ship sailed into the middle of a fishing fleet. Bram, who had been allowed on deck, was sent back into the well at the mainmast. The fishermen gave the distance to Halifax; they were told nothing about Bram or Brown. Through the rest of Monday and into early Tuesday morning, the ship tacked closer to Halifax, until finally at daybreak, after passing through more fog, the harbor appeared. A pilot was spotted and came aboard to bring the *Herbert Fuller* into port, on the morning of the twenty-first, a week after the murders.

⋘⋙

LESTER WAITED ANXIOUSLY for his father's arrival. "He became very nervous as time passed, and his hands shook and dark circles blackened his eyes." On the morning of the twenty-second, though, after a good night's sleep in the city marshal's private office, Monks's first long sleep in a week, he was all talk again, again to the *Boston Globe*.

It was, wrote Thomas F. Anderson, the *Globe* reporter who interviewed Monks at some length in the police chief's office, a "rather disjointed narrative," not a roughly chronological account, like the previous day's report. (Anderson, a Boston newspaperman since the late 1880s, had unusual access in Halifax, where he was born in 1865.)

"Young Monks," the reporter observed in preface, "is an exceedingly good looking and frank appearing young fellow, and a typical Harvard man in tone and action." How this reflected on Monks depended on one's opinion of typical Harvard men, though Monks apparently had neglected to specify that he was a *former* typical Harvard man.

A full night's sleep after a week had restored him. "I never really knew the true value of sleep until last night. To go eight days and nights without any is hard enough, but when it is accompanied, as in my case, by the knowledge that in wakefulness alone lies the hope of life, the mental and physical condition of one who suffers is scarcely to be described." Spencer, in fact, slept less than Monks, but Monks had little to say about him.

"I do not, of course, know," Monks continued, "just how long a period elapsed between the time I was awakened by what I believe was Mrs. Nash's screams and the time I reached the deck and confronted the first mate, but it could only have been a very few minutes and the very most, not more than 10."

Monks acknowledged that this would not have been enough time for Bram, if he was the killer, to have gone aft to consult with Brown: "Here is a seeming mystery that I am not prepared to explain, and at the present moment I could not say definitively on my oath just who killed the three victims, although morally certain of his identity."

"I firmly believe that it was Bram," Monks then asserted, "and I also believe that the superinduced cause was whisky." Liquor is something about which Monks was well schooled.

Was Bram a drinker? Not historically: "He wasn't a drinking man himself," New York shipping agent William Whicker would say. "I've seen him around here weeks at a time, and never saw him take more than a glass of beer at a time, and that was very seldom."

In any case, Monks said he suspected that Brown was somehow involved but for some reason said nothing for days. "This reticence, to my mind, I could not possibly understand, and do not know how any man could keep such a horrible secret so long, and give no indication that he was the possessor of it. It may be, however, that the man was simply a coward, and that his fears of possible consequences to himself were sufficient to restrain him." Indeed.

The helmsman Brown himself, said Monks, could not have left his position to do the killings. "The wind was aft abeam and in that case even a momentary neglect of the helm would have brought the bark about." Dozens of ship captains would eventually testify about how long the ship would hold its course.

The reporter mentioned talk that Bram may have intended to take over the ship and sell it to insurgents in Cuba, where the unrest that soon prompted the famous American invasion was brewing. "I doubt," said Monks, "if Bram, who certainly has some intelligence, very seriously considered the feasibility of such a course. It would have been very easy to convince the seamen, who were a mixed and rather ignorant lot, that such a scheme could be worked, but Bram himself must have known that the thing was practically impossible."

Monks wasn't shy about his opinion of the crew. "If it all had the effect upon me it did, what must it have had upon the super-stitious fears and fancies of the sailors themselves? As time wore on this feeling grew upon them, and some of them were in a ver-itable panic over the imagined groans and screams they heard at night." There actually is no evidence of that.

The *Globe* reporter observed that Monks's experience sounded like one of W. Clark Russell's sea stories. "Well, now, that brings up another strange coincidence," Monks replied, without men-tion of a first strange coincidence, "for the very evening before the murder I had been reading one of Clarke [*sic*] Russell's stories, in which a lot of Malays rise up and murder the captain of the vessel. I little dreamed that within a few short hours I myself would be an actor in an almost similar tragedy." Monks didn't specify his role. Nor, apparently, had he closely read Russell's factual account. It was just two Manila sailors who mutinied, killing both mates and several crewmen before setting the ship on fire and, after being shot by the wounded captain, jumping overboard. In one of the ship's boats, the captain, his wife, and their young daughter, with the fourteen remaining crew, made a passage of seven hundred miles to St. Helena and eventually, by Cunard steamer, back to New York. The heroic captain, who had been jailed for brutality to a previous crew, was quite alive and comfortably retired in 1896. Later, Monks strangely would say that he didn't remember saying anything to the reporter.

If he was confused about the story he was reading in the hours before the murders, Monks was clear that being armed saved him.

"If I had not had my revolver with me when I reached the deck, after discovering the slaying of Capt. Nash, I should probably have been the fourth victim." How that is so is unclear. "The fact that I had the revolver with me," he continued, "I owed to a sudden impulse. Just before I started on what I thought was to be such an enjoyable and health-giving trip, I happened to think of the desirability of getting a revolver. At first I had decided not to get one, but happening to be near a gun store in Boston, and having some spare change, I went in and purchased the firearm. That fact unquestionably explains why I am here today a live man." But a dishonest one; in fact, as he would ultimately acknowledge, his uncle had provided the gun.

Monks's grandiose lying to the *Globe* reporter about the gun suggests that other parts of Monks's story might also be invented. His inversion of the truth about the *Thayer*'s Captain Clarke—he was a heroic survivor, not a pathetic victim—suggests a psychological blockage about the *Fuller*'s captain. Both were strong men capable of violence, but the one in the book Monks was reading was the survivor and the one who slept a few feet from Monks was the victim.

In all of the long interview, as in Monks's account of the previous day, there was not a word of feeling for the victims, especially Charles and Laura Nash, the couple with whom Monks had shared meals, a cabin, and a measure of social equality. Lester's comments were all about his own miraculous escape and nothing about the tragic loss of life. Narcissism hadn't quite been invented yet—Freud's paper introducing the modern psychological concept was published in 1914—but Lester M. would have made a fine patient.

That was it for Lester's free speech. The elder two Monkses arrived in Halifax very late on the twenty-second and went immediately to the jail. "The strain on young Monck [*sic*] has been so great that he broke completely down at the meeting with his father, and he went into a dead faint. Stimulants had to be administered to revive him." After that, Lester was entirely under the control of his relatives and attorney Forbes. His public statements to reporters ceased.

On the morning of the twenty-third, the US consul general in Halifax, Darius Ingraham, started taking evidence from the *Fuller* survivors. Ingraham (1837–1923), a Maine native and former Portland mayor, had been appointed to the Halifax position by President Cleveland in 1893. It was a job that rarely called for much effort or expertise. Indeed, Ingraham and everyone else were quite "at sea regarding the question of proper legal procedure." Thus, numerous people were present for the rounds of questioning, including several city officials and the entire Monks brigade: Lester, his father, his uncle, and his lawyer, Forbes. In fact, Ingraham invited Forbes, whom he knew well from his several years in Halifax, to participate in the questioning. Ingraham later explained: "I stated to Mr. Forbes that, as he was counsel for Mr. Monks and as these prisoners had no counsel, that it might be the interest of justice if he thought of any question which might further the interest of justice that he could ask, as well for the benefit of the prisoner as for the public." As to the fact that Forbes had been hired to protect Lester's interests and that it might conflict with the interests of others, Ingraham shrugged. "Well, I had no particular thought about that."

It was Ingraham's job to conduct the interview of Bram, as with the others, but he let Forbes take over for the questioning of Bram. It was, Ingraham admitted, "quite a lengthy deposition." Finally, after making no objection to any of Forbes's questions, Ingraham just seemed to get tired of them: "I said finally I thought the questions were unnecessary, that it made a prolongation of it."

Precisely what questions Forbes put to Bram is unrecorded. But to a reporter afterward, Bram said, "Yes, I have stated that it was not I who committed the murders, and I feel that the matter will be cleared in a short time, and it will then be shown that I am innocent. I have nothing to fear." Apparently, Bram felt unthreatened by Forbes's questions. For his part, Forbes apparently gained enough information to protect his client.

Alone among the survivors, who were merely questioned, Monks submitted a sworn statement to the US consul general, prepared with Forbes's oversight, on the twenty-third. Two minor curiosities appear at the top. Monks identifies himself as "Student," which he no longer was, and he is misidentified as being from "Brooklyn" in Massachusetts, strangely conflating the Brookline boy with the Brooklyn mate. But the great curiosity is the statement itself, substantially in conflict with Monks's prior statements to reporters.

> I retired to my cabin about 8 o'clock on the evening of the 13th, being very tired, leaving the captain reading in the chart room. I did not notice Mrs. Nash in the cabin, at the time.
>
> I was awakened suddenly from my sleep and sat up in bed. I afterwards learned from the man at the wheel, that this would be 2 o'clock in the morning of the 14th. After being fully awakened, I distinctly heard a woman's cry, and a gurgling noise, like heavy breathing.
>
> I reached for my pistol and also cartridges to load it with, the pistol then being unloaded. [B]efore unlocking my own door leading to the chart room, I called out "Captain Nash" several times, the room where I slept being near the chart room where I had left the Captain reading, but I received no answer. I loaded my pistol and went out into the after cabin.
>
> The only light showing came from a lantern hung from the ceiling in the main cabin and by the dim light I noticed the Captain lying on the floor and breathing heavily, with his cot upturned on its side. I then, in my nightclothes, went to the captain's room and put my hand on him, to arouse him. Thinking he had

injured himself in falling off his cot, I hastened to Mrs. Nash's room to arouse her.

I found her cabin door, leading to the main cabin, opened. I stepped inside the door and noticed the bed clothes in disorder. Large dark patches, in the dim light, showed on the bedclothes. I did not see Mrs. Nash. Noticing on closer viewing that these patches might be blood patches, I at once suspected the cause of the cry which I had heard while in my room. I then left Mrs. Nash's cabin and went aft towards the after companionway. I then stopped, thinking that I might be assaulted and killed in going up the companionway. I turned around and went forward and stood in the companionway in the forward hatch. I there saw the mate pacing up and down, just after the mainmast. I pointed my revolver at him and said something; he then [threw] a piece of board at me.

On the afternoon of the twenty-fourth, Ingraham announced that Monks was "exonerated from all blame" and freed. The three Monkses proceeded quickly to the *Herbert Fuller* and gathered Lester's belongings, including his liquor from the storage room. As he was no longer considered a suspect, no one in authority accompanied them. The contents of his bags were never examined, including the pajamas he was wearing ten nights earlier.

The public, meanwhile, not privy to the details of the investigation, was left to speculate. One question in particular was still being asked: "Many persons have asked how it is that the passenger slept up to the time Mrs. Nash was being killed." The question would go unanswered.

While Monks escaped serious inquiry, Spencer emerged as a hero to some. "Somebody ought to erect a monument to that man," Detective Nicholas Power told a *Boston Herald* reporter on the twenty-third. "It was one of the best pieces of work imaginable. If it had not been for Spencer there is no telling what might have happened." Power's opinion was not enough to free Spencer from confinement.

More quickly than he might have, Detective Power decided what happened on the *Fuller*. This was typical. Over a long career, Power imagined himself a great crime solver, a proto–Sherlock Holmes. In fact, he was more of a proto-Clouseau, though Clouseau, while bumbling, always got the right man; Power, equally self-impressed, usually got the wrong man. When he died in 1938, age ninety-five and long retired, he was carefully described in the local paper as "the most colorful police figure Canada has ever produced." Power's career highlights were mostly major errors in black-and-white. In 1876, he became convinced two visiting Americans were responsible for a local bank robbery. The case against them contained no physical evidence, no witnesses, and no recovered money; neither the Americans nor anyone else was ever convicted. Power showed no interest in a bank official who, days after the theft, left suddenly for England. In 1883, Power famously arrested and interrogated two Irish Americans he believed were planning to assassinate Britain's Prince George, the future King George V, aboard a royal yacht in Halifax Harbour. The suspects had dynamite, diving suits, and related apparatus. As it turned out, the men knew nothing about the prince; they were headed to jobs in local coal mines.

In 1896, Power had a third opportunity to nail an American suspect. He had Bram brought to him for questioning. This was before questioning of Bram by the American consul and after Power had questioned Monks and Brown. Bram arrived chained; Power personally stripped him.

"Bram," Power began, "we are trying to unravel this horrible mystery. Your position is rather an awkward one. I have had Brown in this office and he made a statement that he saw you do the murder."

"He could not have seen me," Bram replied. "Where was he?"

"He states he was at the wheel," said Power.

"Well, he could not see me from there."

Power pressed: "Now look here, Bram, I am satisfied that you killed the captain, from all I have heard from Mr. Brown. But some of us here think you could not have done all that crime alone. If you had an accomplice you should say so, and not have the blame of this horrible crime on your own shoulders."

"Well," Bram replied, "I think and many others on board of the ship think that Brown is the murderer, but I don't know anything about it."

Whether Bram's statement to Power contained an implicit admission of guilt ("he could not have seen me") or a profession of innocence ("I don't know anything about it") would be contested for years to come.

Reports of Power's interview with Bram quickly found their way into the press, via Power, of course. "The police are apparently satisfied that the mate, Thomas Bram, is the perpetrator," reported the *New York Times*, "and believe that they will have but little difficulty in fastening the crime on him."

Bram, for his part, denied it: "I assure you I did not commit the murders. Brown was the only one who could have committed the murders." He told the Halifax police chief, "Tom Bram has neither part nor lot in this murder case. I am, as it were, cast into the den of lions, and I am glad to say that the same God that delivered Daniel is able to deliver me, and will deliver me."

Late on the twenty-third had come word from US authorities that indeed any trials would be held in Boston and that all of the *Fuller* survivors were to be transported there as soon as possible. "Although he did not fear the issue of a fair trial anywhere," reported one paper that day, Bram had one concern if he wound up on trial in Boston: "In his opinion the citizens of Boston would be prejudiced against him owing to the fact that a Boston man had played so prominent a part in the case."

Meanwhile, faith in Brown as a witness took a hit. A reporter spoke to him at length on the twenty-fourth; the next day's headline was "BROWN A MADMAN?" Word of his Rotterdam event had gotten out, and Brown confirmed it. "The question which naturally arises now," asked the paper, "is, was there any derangement of Brown's faculties at the time of that horror on board the Herbert Fuller." Brown, like Bram, remained locked up.

So did supposed hero Spencer, a situation that drew the attention of Boston's Dr. John Dixwell. Dixwell was a brother-in-law of Oliver Wendell Holmes, Jr. and the son of a prominent lawyer who had been master of the Boston Latin School. Like many in this story, Dixwell had been educated at Harvard. As an undergraduate, Dixwell had studied geology under Nathaniel Shaler who, a quarter century later, oversaw the end of Lester Monks's higher education. As a prominent Bostonian, Dixwell was deeply involved in social philanthropies and had been following the *Fuller* case closely since the news broke, particularly the unfairness to Spencer. "It is the irony of fate," Dixwell told the *Boston Globe*, "that because this poor colored man is utterly without friends he should not be shown that same equality before the law which the Halifax authorities have already accorded to Monks."

Dixwell had wired Lester's uncle (whom he knew as a fellow doctor) in Halifax, asking him "to make every effort possible" to get Spencer released; Dixwell offered to furnish bail in any amount. Dr. Monks did not reply, and Dixwell awaited the crew's return to Boston. Canadian authorities had no authority to hold them. The crimes had happened on an American ship in international waters.

A steamer brought the entire contingent from Halifax to Boston. All of the *Fuller* survivors were technically under arrest, but their travel conditions varied, from Bram, relaxed and "neatly dressed" but handcuffed and locked in a storeroom, to Monks, at liberty with his father, uncle, and lawyer in comfortable staterooms. The steamer arrived at Boston on the morning of the twenty-seventh. The *Boston Globe* hailed Monks as "the boy hero of the bark." As Charley Brown, manacled, went down the gangplank to shore, he and the captain and crew exchanged good-byes. Reaching the bottom of the gangplank to be met by a deputy marshal, Bram held out his manacled hands and said, "Good morning," and then continued for those in range, "I feel first rate, and am glad to get to Boston. I hope this thing will be over quick."

It would not be.

6

TO COURT

It's human to lie. Most of the time we can't even be honest with ourselves. . . . In the end, you can't understand the things men do.

—KICHIJIRO (THE COMMONER), IN RASHOMON, 1950 FILM

True criminals vary in looks and tastes and intelligence and method as widely as the rest of the world does, but they have one invariable characteristic: their pathological vanity.

—JOSEPHINE TEY, THE SINGING SANDS (1952)

Bram and Brown were arraigned the afternoon they arrived in Boston and then taken off to the Charles Street jail where the rest of the *Fuller* crew were being held as witnesses. The crew were not unhappy to be held: as witnesses, they were to be paid a dollar a day and be fed and housed, soon in a comfortable home, a much better situation than aboard any ship.

Monks was allowed to return immediately with his father to the family home in Brookline. Monks's legal interests were now chiefly in the hands of Alfred Hemenway, a Harvard-educated longtime leader of the Boston bar and one of the most conservative lawyers in the state. The Monks family knew Hemenway; the previous spring, he and his wife vacationed at a Chesapeake Bay resort hotel in Virginia—the Hygeia at Old Point Comfort, where the first African slaves in America were landed in 1619—whose guest list included Lester and his uncle George.

Monks was free, but Spencer remained jailed, for a day. John Dixwell, who had been disappointed that the Monkses did nothing for Spencer in Halifax, posted Spencer's $1,000 bail on the twenty-eighth, and Spencer was freed. Grateful for the doctor's "kindness of heart," Spencer arranged to leave Boston that night to see his anxious wife in Brooklyn. He was not shy in talking to reporters, shrugging off his own bravery but insisting that "I ought to get the insurance money from the insurance company for bringing the vessel into port." He also questioned the focus on Monks's supposed heroics. "I do not think it is fair for people to make so much talk about Monks' navigating the ship to Halifax. All I have got to thank him for is that he loaned me his revolver. With that in my possession I was able to do a good deal."

Spencer then boarded a train to New York, but when he got to Brooklyn, he didn't go first to his pregnant wife but instead went to a boardinghouse at 285 State Street. "He hardly knew what had brought him" to Hattie Bram's home, but she was grateful to see him. Hattie learned during Spencer's visit that her husband "was a negro," a truth that had escaped her in the eleven years of her marriage. This did not seem to upset her, nor that he had not contacted her. She had earlier filed divorce papers but apparently had never followed through. "I expected Tom would write to me, simply because when people get in trouble the first place they think of is usually home." Yet she seemed still in love with him: "Although he left me three times with three helpless children, and I, perhaps may have been foolish to act as I did sometimes when he came back, I would forgive him and we would take up housekeeping again."

Spencer said little during his visit before moving on to a brief reunion with his wife in south Brooklyn. On the thirtieth, he returned by overnight train to Boston.

In the meantime, Bram quickly found a lawyer. James Cotter would not say who had hired him, but it was understood to be the firm that owned the lumber shipped on the *Fuller*. The proprietors of the firm had known Bram for many years and wanted to make sure he was well represented.

James Edward Cotter, "one of the ranking counselors of New England," was an excellent choice. He was born in County Cork, Ireland, in 1847 and, after his mother died young, came to Marlboro, Massachusetts, in 1855 with his father, who came into possession of a small farm. As a boy, Cotter attended local schools and in the summer worked on the farm. For college, he attended the Bridgewater Normal School (now Bridgewater State University) and then studied in the Marlboro office of William B. Gale, a prominent Harvard-educated criminal lawyer. After passing the state bar, Cotter opened a law office in Boston in 1875. His practice flourished, with many notable and successful civil and criminal cases; among the latter, he famously won a dismissal for Anna Makepeace, who shot and killed her husband in 1891. The following year, Cotter was admitted to the US Supreme Court bar. In 1874, he married Mary Ann Welch, the daughter of an Irish immigrant to Bridgewater; they would have five daughters who grew to maturity, but none had children.

"Mr. Cotter had a lovable personality," observed the *Boston Globe* on his death in 1933. "Quiet, yet with a keen sense of humor he could make any party lively by his remarks. He never had unkind words for anyone, and when he heard others criticising some friend he would suggest that they wait until all the facts were learned." Most important, fellow lawyers said that "no man was more thorough in studying his cases than Mr. Cotter." His defense of Bram would be the highlight of Cotter's career, and Bram would be forever thankful to him.

As the case went forward, Cotter would become Bram's court-appointed lawyer, together with a younger lawyer, Asa Palmer French, himself eventually a noted attorney, famous foremost for the Bram case and as appreciated as Cotter by their client. While Cotter was an Irish immigrant of modest means who made good, French was of a family that settled in Braintree, Massachusetts, in 1640.

The son of a prominent lawyer and judge, French was born in 1860, graduated in 1882 from Yale (where he was a member of Skull and Bones), and then graduated from Boston University Law School. After passing the bar, he went into private practice; among his many important positions after the Bram trials, he served as the US attorney for Massachusetts from 1906 to 1914. He married in 1887 and had two children by his wife, Elisabeth. Unlike the Monks *pere et fils*, French *was* related to the author Hawthorne: a Hawthorne cousin by marriage was French's aunt; his library included an autographed copy of *Twice-Told Tales*, given by the author to her and by her to her nephew. Certain aspects of French's family life would become newsworthy many years later, but none of that had any effect on his effective work for Bram.

Through the summer of 1896, before the essential legal action began in the late fall, people were hungry for any *Herbert Fuller* stories, and the newspapers, especially in Boston, were happy to oblige. On August 3, for example, the *Globe* printed a long interview with one Frank Gnirke, a supposed shipmate of Bram's in 1883 aboard the *Lucy Hastings*, a schooner bound from Maine to Mexico.

Gnirke had a lot to say, and the *Globe* reported everything, including Bram's arrival at the ship in Bangor: "The first time we saw him, he drove to the pier where the schooner was lying. He came in great style, accompanied by his wife and driven by a coachman. At first we thought he was the owner of the cargo, until we found out to the contrary." They found out Bram was merely the mate.

It's a colorful story and entirely false. Bram wasn't married in 1883; it was not until two years later when he was working at Dennett's in New York that he met Hattie. Gnirke was a liar; he had never met Bram, nor did Bram ever sail on the *Lucy Hastings*. The *Globe* did spare its source some embarrassment by calling him Gnirke when his name actually was Guirke, an error of inversion likely originating with the typesetter.

Bram, meanwhile, had adjusted well to life in the Charles Street jail, where he was the recipient of considerable female attentions . . . by mail. Scores of sympathetic women "wrote him encouraging letters, sent cards and flowers and presents of various kinds, and there have never been more gushingly sentimental letters received at the jail." Alas, they were read and discarded.

While the crew and the two accused spent the summer locked up, Monks was free to roam. In mid-August, he was the guest of a former Harvard classmate, Dennis Emory, in Cazenovia, the then fashionable lake resort town in upstate New York; Monks had visited Cazenovia before and would again. A reporter for the *Syracuse Herald* caught up with Monks, who, instructed by the Boston district attorney not to talk about the case, felt compelled to say a few words.

"It is all something I would gladly forget," said Monks, "for the notoriety which has come to me through the terrible affair is anything but pleasing. I did what I thought best under the circumstances, and that is all there is about it. I know it spoiled my vacation." So very unfortunate for him. "I expected to be gone a year," he explained. "I love the water and enjoy that sort of travel. I intended to visit England and other places and finish with a trip on a New-Orleans cotton ship." Monks presented as an extended tour what his father prescribed as a forced absence.

"The whole story is like one of Clark Russell's romances," Monks continued, "and when it is told 10 years hence people will hardly believe it." Again, Monks forgot or didn't realize that the romance he referenced was in fact a true and gruesome ship murder. And the story of the *Herbert Fuller* would remain believable for the victims' families and the surviving crew.

In late October, a grand jury was convened in Boston. It was a federal grand jury because crimes at sea are handled in federal circuit court. The prosecutor would be the US attorney Sherman Hoar; Asa French would hold the position a decade later.

Like French, Hoar came from a distinguished American family that settled in Braintree, Massachusetts, in 1640. He was named for his great-grandfather, founding father Roger Sherman. His father, Ebenezer, had been the US attorney general when the Department of Justice was established in 1870.

Many Hoars attended Harvard; Sherman graduated in 1882. While a student he served as the head model for the statue of John Harvard that presides over Harvard Yard (the sculptor, Daniel Chester French, was a distant relative of Asa French). After law school at Harvard, Hoar went into private practice and served a term in Congress before his appointment by President Cleveland as US attorney.

Hoar married twice, his first wife dying young, as did he. Shortly after contracting typhoid fever in the South on a military tour during the Spanish-American War, he died at home in October 1898. Among many eulogizers, James Cotter recalled Hoar's "manly form, his aggressive, earnest and sometimes severe utterances." Cotter also recalled Hoar as a guest in his home: "There he was the amiable gentleman, the light-hearted, genial personality, almost the reverse of what he was to his professional brethren."

Hoar had no doubt who was responsible for the *Herbert Fuller* deaths. Among the witnesses he presented to the grand jury were Monks, Spencer, and members of the crew, including Brown but not Bram.

Monks testified on October 20, reportedly well recovered from his shipboard ordeal. "He has been hunting through the summer in the Adirondacks, and, besides returning with recovered health, he has the antlers of a buck as a proof of his prowess as a hunter."

Spencer testified after Monks and the crew the following day. On the twenty-second, Brown was dismissed as a suspect but held on $5,000 bail, guaranteed to keep him from disappearing. On the thirtieth, Bram was indicted for the murders. On Halloween, Monks played in an eighteen-hole golf tournament at the Brookline Country Club. "The dead leaves over the course interfered with the players, and a large number of balls were lost. Lester Monks was an interesting figure on the course."

If we are trying to understand how Bram could be indicted while Monks was merely interesting, we might consider another interesting young man in the America of 1896. Frederick Hoffman was a German immigrant and, at age thirty-one, a leading statistician with the Prudential Life Insurance Company. In August, after serialization earlier during the year by the American Economic Association, Hoffman's book *Race Traits and Tendencies of the American Negro* was published by Macmillan.

"In the plain language of the facts," wrote Hoffman, "the colored race is shown to be on the downward grade, tending toward a condition in which matters will be worse than they are now, when diseases will be more destructive, vital resistance still lower, when the number of births will fall below the deaths, and gradual extinction of the race take place." Unfortunately, for the time being, "the presence of the colored population is a serious hindrance to the economic progress of the white race." Fortunately, "gradual extinction is only a question of time."

As horrifying and wrong as Hoffman's conclusions and predictions were, they were quite popular in their time, both within the life insurance industry that needed justification for charging blacks the same as whites for much less coverage and in the general population of passive racists, ardent eugenicists, and, eventually, Nazis.

In the trial ahead, Spencer was openly identified as Negro, while Bram was suspected: "In his talk he was not unlike Spencer, there being a suspicion of the negro, but his voice was stronger and clearer and his delivery was not so rapid," vocal strength, clarity, and pacing apparently being race traits of whites.

Monks had his own association with a black person. His landlady during his second year at Harvard was a Mrs. Torrey, at 18 Plympton Street, near campus. For whatever reason, Monks's lawyers, Hemenway and Forbes, saw fit to visit her before the trial and instruct her not to give any information about Monks while he was her tenant. What information she might have had is unknown. Bram's lawyers never investigated what secrets she might have held.

Another person who would not figure at Bram's trial was Francis Bartlett, a Monks family attorney. Monks's father considered it wise to send Lester to the family lawyer, out of concern over "the identity of the murderer and not unmindful of the impression the young man's personal record might make on the jury." At the least, the fact that Lester was a drunk who had just been thrown out of Harvard might not have played well in court.

Bartlett was a Harvard graduate (1857) and the son of one, Sidney (1818). Sidney Bartlett had been the leader of the Boston bar; Francis was better noted as an art collector and benefactor, eventually gifting millions of dollars in money, property, and Greek and Roman sculpture to Massachusetts institutions. As a lawyer, he primarily offered private counsel, rather than legally serving as one. By the time Lester showed up at his office in 1896, Bartlett's life had been touched by much sadness. His wife had died in 1873 after less than six years of marriage, and their younger of two daughters had died at age nine in 1881. The remaining child, Caroline, would marry well and have two daughters herself, but she suffered with "melancholia" for years. Eventually, in 1908, she would jump from a window in her suite of rooms on the thirteenth floor of the St. Regis Hotel on Fifth Avenue in New York City; her face and head were crushed beyond recognition. Francis Bartlett became his family's only survivor.

Bartlett had read all the newspaper reports in advance of Lester's visit, but he needed to hear the story directly from Lester. He seated Lester in a chair next to his desk and said, "Now tell me the entire story." The twenty-year-old felt comfortable with the sixty-year-old who as a frequent guest in the Monks home had watched Lester grow up. Lester spoke for two hours, increasingly confident and comfortable as he related the terrible story.

When he finished, he looked up and noticed the lawyer's head was in his hands. Bartlett seemed lost in anguished thought. Finally, Bartlett asked, "Is that all?" Lester, thinking he had done well, said yes. Bartlett swiveled his chair toward Lester, placing a hand on young Monks's shoulder, and said, "My boy, tell me why you did it." Lester's response is not recorded.

THOUGH THREE PEOPLE were killed, prosecutor Hoar opted, for the trial at hand, to try Bram only for the murder of Captain Nash. Though the indictment was for all three victims, Nash's was the only death with a supposed witness, Brown. Hoar kept open the possibility of trying Bram later for the other two deaths.

Bram's trial started on December 14 with jury selection. Anticipation was high. "It will be one of the most remarkable murder cases known in this part of the country," observed the *Boston Herald*, noting that the case lacked only one major item: a motive.

The trial was in the hands of two federal judges, district judge Nathan Webb (1825–1902) and circuit judge LeBaron Bradford Colt (1846–1924).

Colt knew something about weaponry and the law. For well over two decades after the 1862 death of his uncle Samuel, teams of Colts battled each other through many courts all the way to the Supreme Court over the famous gunmaker's substantial estate. LeBaron and his immediate family eventually got nothing for their efforts, but in the meantime he graduated from Yale (where he, like Asa French after him, was a Bonesman) and Columbia Law and then became a prominent lawyer in Rhode Island, a federal district judge, and, in 1891, a judge on the newly created Court of Appeals for the First Circuit.

Webb graduated from Harvard the year Colt was born and went on to an unremarkable law career in his hometown, Portland, Maine, before his appointment in 1882 to the federal district court of Maine, the position he held until the year of his death.

As the handlers of Thomas Bram's murder trial, the aging Webb would mostly defer to the younger but judicially senior Colt. The roles of both judges would be secondary to the performances of the accused, the principal witnesses, and the attorneys for the defense and prosecution.

The jury was chosen without much fuss in a little more than two hours, without getting past *J* in the pool:

Henry Arnold, lumber-mill owner, from Adams, declined appointment as foreman due to rheumatism in arm

Warren Blake, retired leather manufacturer, Woburn; his sister would die during the trial

Harry Booth, commercial traveler, Hyde Park, had employed Cotter six years earlier in a civil case

Oliver Briggs, carpenter and builder, Cambridge, the only Mason on the jury

Robert Brown, farmworker, West Newbury

Edward Burke, florist, Boston, son of a Boston police inspector

Sheperd Dyer, fireman, Plainfield, a Civil War veteran

Abel Ford, no profession, Hyde Park; like Booth, Ford was a former Cotter client

Stephen Green, shoemaker, Stoneham

Charles Howes, sailmaker, Chatham, eventually the last sailmaker on Cape Cod

John Hughes, stonemason, Adams
Rinaldo Jack, traveling flour and cereal salesman, Boston, named
    the foreman after Arnold declined

It was a jury of Bram's peers in that the jurors were all men.
That's where any similarities stopped. They were all white and
American born. The jurymen were paid two dollars a day (twice
the *Fuller* crew witnesses) plus seventy-five cents for food per
diem and were lodged in one large room on cots at the famous
Quincy House, then downtown Boston's largest hotel.

In his opening statement, Hoar felt compelled to warn the jurors
about one of the witnesses who would appear before them: "Spencer is a colored man, and we might just as well start right out by
knowing the kind of people we have to deal with." Whether Bram
also was colored would be left to the imaginations of the jurors.

The prosecution would call nearly thirty witnesses, a number
of them various officials testifying only briefly to establish basic
facts, but most important all of the *Fuller* survivors but for the defendant. The defense most notably would call Bram and numerous
old sea captains on whether a ship such as the *Fuller* could maintain its course with the wheel lashed; the defense would point
relentlessly to Brown as the murderer and somewhat less avidly
to Monks. The witnesses who mattered the most were the three
men aboard the *Fuller* physically closest to the victims: the accused Bram, the supposed witness Brown, and the murder cabin's
lone survivor, Monks.

"To me killing isn't a matter of such great consequence as you
might think." Monks actually didn't say that; neither did Bram or
Brown. The bandit Tajomaru did, in his confession in Ryūnosuke
Akutagawa's "In a Grove," the 1921 short story that inspired Akira
Kurosawa's film *Rashomon*. In the story, Tajomaru is among several main characters who, in extended monologues before a mag-
istrate, give differing versions, for varying reasons, of a samurai's

violent death in a secluded grove. Akutagawa wants the reader to accept that truth may be unknowable (the movie version is less inscrutable).

Like readers of the short story, we cannot know what happened in the early morning of July 14, 1896, on the *Herbert Fuller* in the remote Atlantic. We can only read what various people aboard the ship said—in distillations of their court testimony—and decide for ourselves.

Brown's story, as told to the prosecution:

I went on watch at midnight. Before the watch I had slept on deck, on top of the forward house under the longboat. I slept there because there were lots of insects in the forecastle. At midnight, I took the wheel from Oscar Anderson.

I first saw the first mate after I had been to the wheel for a couple of minutes. He talked with the second mate for a few minutes forward of the mizzen on the starboard side, then the second mate went below. After that, for about an hour, I saw the first mate walking thwartships from one side to another. Sometimes I lost him from my sight. He walked over to the port side, and where he went I don't know. I couldn't see. He was gone from sight about five or six minutes.

The third time I lost sight of him on deck I saw him down in the cabin. I hear some noise first. I was scared and took a jump to myself. I looked through the window on the back of the cabin. I saw the bed there was upset. The bed the captain was sleeping in. I saw the man lying down on the floor. I could see about half his body, from his feet up.

I looked at my compass to see if my vessel was on her course and then looked again through the window. I saw somebody standing in the cabin. It was mate Bram. In a dark suit of clothes and a straw hat. A common straw hat with a small hole in the upper part of it. Mate Bram wore that hat every day. I saw him lift a weapon. I could not say what kind of a weapon it was. I saw the handle. It looked to be an axe, with a long handle. I saw a blow fall in the same direction of the Captain's head. I did not see Bram holding the weapon, just the blow fall. Then he walked right out of the room, so I be awfully scared and nervous. I watched the after companionway. I thought he should come up. Then I heard a scream from Mrs. Nash. Next I saw mate Bram on deck, on the starboard side between main and mizzen rigging. It was just a little time after I heard the scream.

Brown's story, as told to the defense:

I went to the wheel at twelve o'clock. It was a cloudy night; a cloudy heaven and dark. The door of the after companionway was open. The curtain over the window was slide to one side, slide away from the window. There were no bars outside the glass of the window. I hold on to the wheel with both hands. Never took them off. The vessel was running fast.

There was light enough in the cabin for me to see the man inside the window. I didn't know that the captain occupied that room. I thought always Mr. Monks occupied that room. At half past one I see trouble in the room. The time I hear a noise first got my attention. It was the bed that the captain was sleeping in, upset. I did nothing, just jumped, scared myself. Kept hold of the wheel, with both hands. I put my eyes to the compass and I pulled over the helm a couple of spokes to keep my vessel on her course. I see somebody standing right up against the window, inside. The clothes were dark except the hat, which were white. He stand there only for a few seconds.

I know that somebody been murdered. I did not say a word. Did not alarm anybody. Did not ring the bell at the binnacle. Only ring the bell to get orders. It was too late for me to save the captain at the time I saw it. I could have sung out as much as I liked, I could do anything I liked, but I saw there was a murder there and I couldn't make as much noise as I liked. I was nervous and scared. I was scared for my own life. I stayed at the wheel for another half hour.

Putting together the essential portions of these two versions, Brown said he saw a single blow and that Bram was there for only a few seconds. But the captain took seven blows to the head, which would take considerably more time even if done without pause. Possibly Brown saw only the final blow; possibly also he was lying about the details of what he saw or even about seeing anything at all. In other parts of his testimony, he acknowledged that he "spin[s] lots of yarns," and that "I tell lots of yarns." He admitted that his oft-told shipboard story of having killed a man in Rotterdam was "a lie; that is only a story." The trial transcriber noted that this admission caused "Sensation in the court room." Possibly his testimony about Bram was also "only a story."

Bram's story, as told to the defense:

I looked at the clock, at the steps leading down from the deck to the forward companionway, and it showed two o'clock or a couple of minutes after, and I sung out to Brown at the wheel, "Four bells." I got no reply. I turned around and Frank Loheac came along. I said to him, "Four bells." He says, "Four bells, sir." I went ahead of him aft to the wheel. I saw Brown stopping [sic] down putting his slippers on. Loheac relieved him and Brown took a bucket from outside of the after house and went forward with it. Then I walked around the mizzenmast and looked to leeward and faced aft.

In facing aft, I saw someone standing in the forward compan-ionway with a revolver pointing at me. The revolver was bran[d] new, nickel plated, and shined. I didn't hesitate. I picked up a piece of board and held the board in front of me. Mr. Monks says, "Who is that?" Says I, "It is me." I stood over the companionway with that board in front of me, and he says, "Come down here." Says I, "What is wrong?" Says he, "Come down here, Mr. Bram, don't be afraid, it is me; the captain is killed." Says I, "What!" With scare, thinking that I was far enough away from the com panionway, I let the board drop, and it slid right down the steps and went down to the bottom of the stairway. I went down, and going down I throwed this piece of board back on deck.

Mr. Monks says, "Come to my room with me till I get some clothes on." In going to his room I took the lamp down, or Mr. Monks took it down, I don't just remember. It was turned on a half light, just light enough to show the time on the clock. I turned the lamp up bright and in entering the cabin, sure enough, the captain lay there dead, or very near dead. Once in a while there would be a kind of gurgling. Quite a while afterwards there would be another one. And seeing this I went over to his feet and felt of his feet and his feet was cold. With that I ran back into Monks' room and stationed myself by the door and kept peeping on the outside, looking all around while Monks put his clothes on.

Monks says, "I will be ready in a little while." When Monks was ready I says, "Let us go into Mrs. Nash's room now and see Mrs. Nash's room." He says, "It ain't no use going there. I have been there; she is dead already. Don't lose any time in this cabin; there is too many holes around."

I was scared myself and I left the lamp burning in Mr. Monks' room on a full blast, lighting up this chart room where the captain slept. I left the lamp in the same position and Monks and I came up on deck.

We were stationed close to the mizzen rigging to windward. While we stayed there, I was thinking of the sight that I seen down in the cabin, I got sick to my stomach, throwed up a little, close to where I was. And Monks and I stood there and said I, "Mr. Monks, this is very funny." Monks said to me, "Where is the second mate?" Says I, "It is his watch below; ain't he in his room?" He said, "I didn't see him." "Well," I said, "if he is not down there he is forward with the men. Monks, let us go forward and wake the steward up." He says, "Don't either you nor I leave this station

here, because we don't know who is under these boats forward."
"Well," said I, "I think it is better to get someone else with us than
to be alone." Said he, "We will wait until daylight and call the
steward." Said I, "All right, we won't move then."

Bram's tale, as told to the prosecution:

At one o'clock I went down and took a drink and got the sandwich that the steward had laid there for me the same night at
seven o'clock. I came up on deck and ate the sandwich.

I saw the form of a man and a revolver pointed, a shining
revolver, pointed direct to me. At first I didn't recognize him. He
was leaning on my door at the foot of the steps, leaning forward.
Mr. Monks had his shoulder up against my door and the second mate's room door was right abreast of him, and the revolver
pointed up the companionway, and I stood over the companionway looking down, with the board shielding myself. Picked it up
as soon as I saw the revolver in his hand.

When he said to me, "Come down," I said, "What is wrong?"
and he said, "It is me—come down, the captain is killed." With
scare, I dropped the board, from over the steps to the deck load,
down into the steps of the forward companionway, but not at
Mr. Monks. When I dropped the board on Monks, I was standing sort of looking down the companionway.

He was right ahead of me, we were right close together. I
seen the Captain lying dead bleeding. I think he was dead.
Mr. Monks, he said he was dead, and he appeared to be. Once
or twice he gave this noise. I saw him bleeding. I felt of his feet.
They were cold. The Captain was helpless then. I didn't stay out
in that cabin at all. I had my head out through his door looking
into the dark forward cabin where there was not any light. I was
not looking any particular place for anybody, but I thought, to
guard ourselves, we might probably see something or hear something. Somebody could have come out of the water closet, which

is directly through the chart room, there might have been somebody in there. Mr. Monks and I never lost any time in that cabin
that night.

Before leaving his room I suggested to Mr. Monks "Let us
go into Mrs. Nash's room." He said, "No use going in there, for
I have been in there already and she is dead. Let us get up out
of here."

When we got to my room Mr. Monks faced me. It was dark
then, no light then, and his back was turned to the second mate's
room. I unlocked my trunk and got my revolver, with cartridges
that was in this mitt, and we both went on deck. There was nothing said about the second mate then by any of us until we got on
deck. The lantern was left in Mr. Monks room, in full blaze by
the door. I did not take it out of the room; I left it there on the
floor. At the time that Mr. Monks and I were down there, I was
so perplexed, and so was Mr. Monks himself. It was probably lack
of judgment on my part to leave the lantern. I cannot justify myself in doing it, no, sir, because at that moment it was a very hard
thing to tell what to do.

Mr. Monks asked me shortly after we got on deck, "Where is
the second mate?" I said, "Ain't he in his room? "I didn't see him,"
he said. "Well," I said, "if he ain't down there, he is forward." And
I started to walk towards there and Mr. Monks called me back to
stay with him. The first mention was on deck. That is the time I
made a move to go along, but Mr. Monks said, "Don't go," and I
came back. I wasn't extra anxious of going there myself. A revolver
ain't all that a man needs in a case of that sort. I suppose I lacked
grit, courage. He was anything but in a right steady state of mind.
He was not better than I was at this time. When I make a suggestion, he objects. I would not feel justified in going anywheres
aboard that ship alone out of sight of Mr. Monks. For the simple
reason I was scared myself. He was as bad as I was.

When Monks and I came up to the deck, after I had seen the
condition that the Captain was, I got sick to my stomach from

seeing the sight down below, and throwed up a very little on the weather side between the main and mizzen rigging. There was nothing said about it then. The next morning I went along and we all gathered. Who brought the conversation up I do not just remember, but Mr. Monks says, "You probably might have been drugged." I told Mr. Monks that when I came on deck at twelve o'clock the second mate gave me a drink, and he said that he got it from Mr. Monks. Said I, "I don't think the second mate had any drug in that bottle; what do you know about it?" He says, "Well, you don't know what was in that liquor." And I says, "That didn't make me sick, I don't believe, because there is very little of it throwed up." I never mentioned a word about drugged to Mr. Monks. We came aft and I leaned against this rail. To the best of my recollection my feet slipped someway or other from under me, and I remember the slippers that I had on got into this little bit of stuff, this bread sandwich. It came up of its own free will and accord. I am positive I did not put a finger in my mouth. We stood on the deck there then, and there was nothing more said about it to my knowledge, about analyzation or nothing else. I don't believe that the argument on analyzation ever came up with us. Mr. Monks did not slap me on the back and tell me to brace up or try to keep me awake. That was no time to sleep, I am sure of that. I never staggered on the deck.

I suggested to Mr. Monks we go get the steward, and he said "we had better not go, it is dark, we don't know who is under the boats." I proposed it twice or three times while we stood there, but it was too dark then, Mr. Monks said, and we had better wait till daylight.

Monks's tale, as told to the prosecution:

Well, I remember waking up and hearing a scream. At first I did not pay much attention to it, and then I listened and I heard this sort of gurgling noise coming from where the Captain slept and that—it did not seem to me as though that was natural, and it waked me up completely so that I was wide awake. I listened and I heard some more, and then I called "Captain Nash, Captain Nash," and I got no answer, so I thought I would investigate.

So I set up in my bunk and pulled open the drawer which was right under the bunk, and took from it a box of shells, and I opened the box of shells—it had never been opened—and I got a revolver which I had under my head. Then I got up and put on a pair of slippers and went to the door and unlocked the door, and stepped out in the chart room, as you call it.

I could see some—it was from a lantern which was hanging in the main cabin—and I could see the cot which Captain Nash slept on was tipped over on its side. I could see that Captain Nash was lying on the floor, and I went up to him and put my hand on his shoulder and said "Captain Nash," and he did not answer at all, and this sort of gurgling sound went on. And then I went to Mrs. Nash's room to call her to go to the Captain, and I stepped inside the room there, and I did not see Mrs. Nash, but I saw her bunk, and on the sheets I could see these dark splashes, and I suddenly realized that the scream I heard meant something.

Then I thought I had better get out of the cabin just as quick as I could. I started to go aft and go out of the after companionway, but I thought somebody might be standing on top of the companionway and strike me when I came out from behind. So I turned around and went forward to the forward companionway and looked out on deck, and there I saw Mr. Bram walking up and down between the mainmast and the mizzenmast, from the starboard side to the port side. I don't think it could have been more than 10 minutes since I first awoke.

When I saw Mr. Bram walking up and down there I called to him. I said "Mr. Bram." All the time I had had this revolver in my hand, and when I saw him I pointed it to him and I called "Mr. Bram," and he came a little towards me and picked up a plank and threw it towards me. Instead of going in the hatchway, it went across; it did not come in. I was just inside of the actual companionway, that is to say, just inside the cabin.

Then I called to him, and I said "Come below, the Captain has been murdered," and he said "No, no, no," and I said, "Come below and see for yourself." When I said this I stepped out a little further on the deck, and then we turned around and went down together, and he stopped and went into his stateroom. I don't re-member whether I was in front of him or behind him, but I was quite near him. I did not go into his stateroom. As I remember, I stood just at the threshold of the main cabin.

I told him to get his revolver and he got it, and then he took down took the lantern which hung over the table and went into my stateroom with me. There I slipped off my pajamas and put on a pair of duck trousers and a flannel shirt, and while I was in there he started to go away, and I called him back, and then we went on deck again. When we were below, Mr. Bram did not go near the captain or make any examination of his cabin. He didn't go near Mrs. Nash or in her room and didn't ask any questions about her.

Monks's tale, as told to the defense:

I had a series of colds through the winter for the last two years, colds and a sore throat, &c., and [Dr. Monks, my uncle and phy-sician] thought it would be better for me to take a trip to some warm climate and be away from the New England winter for at least one year. I should not have been home if everything had gone well at that time until the next June anyway. I had a little medicine chest which I have now, a common thing to use with medicines such as headache powders and pills; that is all.

The captain was covered with blood. I didn't know it was blood on his body. I suppose there was not light enough. What

The *Herbert Fuller*, the day after arrival in Halifax, July 21, 1896
(MUSEUM OF NOVA SCOTIA)

Lester Monks, circa mid-1920s (PRIVATE COLLECTION)

Thomas Bram, circa 1927 (NATIONAL ARCHIVES)

The *Herbert Fuller* crewmen, circa 1896; front row: Henry Slice, Hendrik Perdok, Charley Brown, Frank Loheac; back row (between bailiff and deputy marshal): Folke Wassen, Oscar Anderson. There are no reproducible photographs of the Nashes or second mate Blomberg (BOSTON ATHENAEUM)

The *Herbert Fuller* wheel, lashed, and window to chart room, barred
(Museum of Nova Scotia)

The forward companion way, showing five-foot stack of lumber deck load;
entry to Bram's cabin on the left, and to Blomberg's cabin opposite
(Museum of Nova Scotia)

Main section of aft cabin, looking aft: the chart room is rear left; dining table, lantern, and clock are center; aft companionway is right; above left is skylight (MUSEUM OF NOVA SCOTIA)

Aft cabin, starboard side, looking forward; from right: chart room, Monks's room, Mrs. Nash's room, main cabin with heating stove (MUSEUM OF NOVA SCOTIA)

Aft cabin, starboard side, looking forward, close-up: Monks's cabin to right, Mrs. Nash's cabin center; note open door between rooms that was closed and locked during voyage (MUSEUM OF NOVA SCOTIA)

Mrs. Nash's bloodied bed (MUSEUM OF NOVA SCOTIA)

Mrs. Nash's bloodied pillow
(MUSEUM OF NOVA SCOTIA)

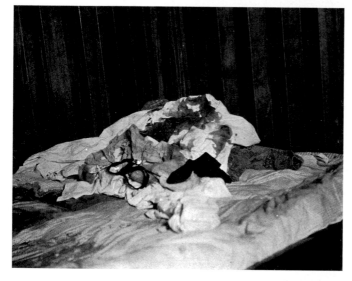

Mrs. Nash's bloodied
bedding and clothes
(MUSEUM OF NOVA SCOTIA)

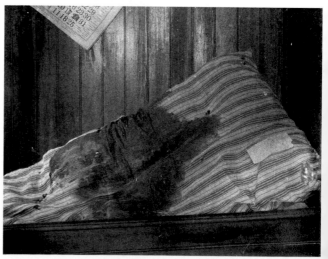

Blomberg's bloodied mattress
(MUSEUM OF NOVA SCOTIA)

JOURNAL from *Boston* towards *Buenos Ayres*

H	K	4	COURSES.	WINDS.	LEEWAY.	Remarks *Monday, 13th day of July*	1896

This day comes in with mod
breeze and smooth seas

at or about 2 A.M. Tuesday
there an alarm made by passenger
Mr. Monks There then was
mutiny on board while none on
deck at the time seen or saw nothing
of what had been done but as
it was my watch on deck myself
and Mr. Monk went down in the
cabin and found that the Capt
and his wife and 2nd mate had
been killed with ax which
Whereon was thrown overboard by
request of Mr. Monks and Steward
As hands was brought aft but
none could account for it
we then concluded to put the vessel
back to the Nearest Port to make
known the same

Course	Distance	Diff. of Lat.	Departure	Lat. by D. R.	Lat. by Ob.	Variation	Diff. of Lon.	Lon. in.	Lon. by Ob.
6	72 E	212	72	162	67	—	16	2 01	58 04

Bram's entry in the *Herbert Fuller* logbook describing "alarm made by passenger Mr. Monks" (BOSTON ATHENAEUM)

Bram, in Boston *Sunday Post*, January 3, 1897

NEW YORK, *U.S. Exhibit 23*
March 20/98
Ars
189

Tuesday. July 14th 1896.

Monday night every-thing on board of the
Barkentine "Herbert Fuller" was perfectly quite
and peaceful. The crew had no fault to find
with any thing on board. The second mate had
the watch from 8 until 12. I went to bed about
8 o'clock, the steward says the captain had been
drinking but I did not notice it. I am naturally
a very heavy sleeper so do not know so the
murders which were committed might have happened
sometime before I woke up.

My first recollections are these: I heard a
scream followed by a gurgling noise as if someone was choking, I reached down and got a box
of shells for my revolver and filled the pistol, which
I kept under my pillow, as fast as possible. Then
I called "Captain Nash"; as I got no answer I unlocked my cabin door and stepped out into the after-
cabin. The Captain slept on a cot placed
against the starboard wall. The Captain was lying

Monks's statement (first page), July 14, 1896, written on hotel stationery provided
by Bram (BOSTON ATHENAEUM)

Monks, circa 1886
("Monks Memorabilia")

Monks, circa 1920
(private collection)

Monks, circa 1925 (private collection)

RECEIVED at

J 80 C GI 43 paid D. P. 3 ex. 1.33p

New York, July 22, '96.

Lester H. Monks,

                    Halifax, N. S.

Will you write story of experiences on board the Fuller for
Sunday Journal in about two thousand words and telegraph it
to-morrow, Thursday evening? Will send you check for such article
at usual magazine rates? Please wire answer my expense.

                        Morrill Goddard, Editor, New York Sunday
                                        Journal.

New York Sunday Journal editor Merrill Goddard's solicitation to Lester Monks, July 22, 1896. Monks never wrote about what happened on the *Fuller,* for the *Journal* or anyone else (PRIVATE COLLECTION)

Boston Sunday Post, January 3, 1897. Note the question for discussion, repeated for many days; the published responses ran heavily to the negative.

Boston Post, January 21, 1897. The diagram shows what were considered the strongest arguments on appeal; the Supreme Court eventually chose a much less heralded basis for their historic 5th Amendment-based reversal

Richard Hale to Eldon James, December 21, 1933, asserting that Monks's trial testimony "was a story made up by himself" (HARVARD LAW SCHOOL LIBRARY, HISTORICAL & SPECIAL COLLECTIONS)

Alfred Worcester to Eldon James, March 27, 1939, refuting Hale's assertion (HARVARD LAW SCHOOL LIBRARY, HISTORICAL & SPECIAL COLLECTIONS)

Monks, circa 1925, in "Hyassa," his Buzzards Bay 15, bought in 1922. Boat—dock line taut and rigging flexed—and owner—impatient and anxious—both seem to be straining for freedom from their attachments. Monks would die in 1927; the boat, with different name and owner, would be lost in the 1938 New England hurricane (PRIVATE COLLECTION)

made me say there was blood on his body, I put my hand on his shoulder and my hand came away all wet, and when the men told me the next day he was all blood I supposed it was blood.

The door leading from my stateroom to the chart room was locked. I used to lock it nights. At other times it was unlocked. The key was in the door.

I was up on deck talking with the two mates. Then I went below and passed by the captain, and said good-night to him, and went to bed. I had no light in my room at all. I stopped reading [the Clark Russell book] just after dinner.

The revolver was given to me by my uncle; wanted to bring a revolver with me. I thought that under my pillow was a good place to keep it. Never loaded.

The captain's loaded revolver was found under the mattress in my room Sunday afternoon after the murders. I had never seen it before.

I saw dark spots against the white sheets. I understand she was away in the inside of the berth. I didn't particularly try to see her. As soon as I saw these dark splashes, I realized that it meant something—the scream I had heard.

If I had gone out of the aft companionway, somebody might have stood right on top of the house and hit me when I came up. In going up the forward way I could see everything forward. They would not have the whole top of the forward way to stand on as they would on the aft way.

The mate was perhaps 20 feet away. I was not surprised to see him there. I don't think he could see the pistol. I had it to shoot him if he tried to hurt me. I wanted to have this whole thing explained to me. When they were killed I was sound asleep. Bram was awake, and I supposed he knew more about it.

When he saw me, I called to Bram. He picked up a board to throw at me, and I called out, "It is me, Mr. Monks. Come below for God's sake." I said, "Come below. The captain has been murdered." Bram came up toward me and said, "No, no." I asked for the second mate, and he said the second mate was forward, and that the crew had mutinied.

We took the lantern down and into my room, directly into my room. He started to go away, and I asked him to come back. I didn't want him roaming around. I wanted to know what he was doing. I thought it was much better for him to be with me. Not because I suspected him. He didn't go up and examine Capt. Nash, at all; he passed right into my room.

I saw a sort of dripping of blood all along the roof of the after house. Most of the blood was around the companionway. From the forward companionway and went across on the port side of the after house on top and there a little way down, oh, I should say perhaps 20 feet, there was a broad place, broad streak of blood, and then going back constantly growing fainter right back to where the axe was found under a deck stringer.

Before the case went to the jury on January 1, there were some notable moments, other than the testimony above, during the two weeks since the trial started.

In his opening statement, prosecutor Hoar said that Brown, on the helm, looking through the aft cabin window, "saw something that looked like the handle of an axe, and he saw the victim and saw what he had on his head, and it was the white straw hat which Thomas Bram had, that had no top to it." Judge Webb had to point out that Hoar had made Bram the victim.

On December 20, during the prosecution's case, Bram was visited in jail by a group of city aldermen and made an extended assertion of his innocence, reported exclusively by the *Globe*:

My conscience says I'm innocent, and nothing in the world will make me afraid. . . . If you had seen that woman's head that morning you would have said no civilized man could have done it. That woman had no head. It seemed as if it was crushed. . . . I want to leave the world straight. I know I am right. The way my captain died, and the way his wife and the second mate died, is awful. . . . I am all alone here. I am an innocent man, and I stand in the presence of God a man with a clear conscience. It is an awful crime, and awful charge. I cannot realize sympathy with a man who can brutalize people like that. I say no man in his sane mind could do it. There was prejudice against me. So far they have got mixed up on the testimony. God only knows how this will come out. I trust him. I am happy, for I am all right. The people in Boston are surprised at me. I smile and laugh, they say. I cannot help it. My conscience is clear, and I am confident that I am going to walk the streets of Boston a free man. . . . [W]hen we first came here [to Boston] . . . it was said that I wanted to wreck the bark and take the cargo. So far no evidence has come out as to that. I never made any suggestion but what was approved by all hands. The idea of a man taking a civilized country's property: taking a load of lumber and going away and stealing it! I don't believe there is a true-hearted man in Boston who can believe Brown's statement. . . . I need sympathy, and have it from a good many. If I was a guilty man I would not look for it.

Attorney Cotter got Monks on the witness stand to say, of his encounter with the dying Nash, "I put my hand on his shoulder and my hand came away all wet, and when the men told me the next day he was all blood I supposed it was blood." But Cotter failed to pursue the obvious problem with Monks's assertion: if his hand was wet from blood, Monks wouldn't have needed a day to know it. His hand would have been red. The blood would have been transmitted from his hand to whatever he touched . . . unless he cleaned it off, which he must have done before he went forward to find Bram.

Also, the captain's head was a bloodied pulp. It is impossible that if Monks was close enough to feel blood on the captain's shoulder that Monks didn't also notice that the head on which the shoulder rested had been bashed by many axe blows. It is a mystery why Cotter did not pursue this as well.

Attorney French, in his statement opening the defense, asked, "How it is possible that when the axe had struck seven times into a living body and had been seven times lifted and thrown down over the man's shoulder toward his head—above his head, with the fury which that demon must have used, how is it possible that he did not become absolutely spattered and covered with blood?" Bram's clothes had no blood on them, and he wore them for five days after the killings.

Cotter's closing featured an extended attack on Monks:

The testimony of Mr. Monks is not entitled to credence. [It is] singular that Monks, down in that room, with all that cutting and chopping, didn't hear more than what he testified to.

The moment he strikes Halifax he is under the advice of counsel; his statement is prepared by counsel; his father and his uncle and other distinguished people are present before the American consul. He is the only person who acts under the advice of counsel, the only person whom counsel is assisting. For what purpose? Charged with no offence, charged with no crime, and the counsel selected by him undertakes to cross-examine Bram and to fasten this offence upon Bram!

[I]t was singular, that this man should occupy an apartment with only a frail partition between him and Captain Nash on the one side and Mrs. Nash on the other side, a doorway leading from his apartment to either room, whether locked or unlocked, the second mate's room only a few feet away, and that these three people, these three persons, were chopped, battered, with marks on the ceiling and on the partitions, on the one side and the other of this man, and he was never aroused, never heard the occurrence, until it was all over with, and he heard the outcry of this woman; then went on deck with a revolver in his hand and the

Captain's revolver under his mattress. Bram was justified in saying "It is singular he doesn't know more about this occurrence than what he has told."

[W]hatever else may be said of Lester Hawthorne Monks, the offence which he committed in this court . . . for the purpose of injuring the cause of this defendant, is nothing short of deliberate perjury. . . . [W]hen a man selects his position for the purpose of relieving himself from suspicion, for the purpose of convicting somebody else . . . it cannot be described by any other term than direct and downright perjury. He has been misleading in every attitude taken by him in this case wholly for the purpose of satisfying his own vanity.

WHATEVER THE DEFENSE hoped to gain by attacking Monks, it failed, though it took a while and stunned most observers. "The Verdict a Surprise to Almost Everybody," ran one of the headlines in the *Boston Sunday Herald*. On January 2, after deliberating for more than a day, the jury returned. They had taken at least a dozen votes, ranging from eleven to one to seven to five, all favoring guilt, before returning with the required unanimous guilty verdict. The vote just before the final one was nine to three. On the final vote, the last of the holdouts—reportedly sailmaker Charles Howes—said, "May God forgive me and have mercy on my soul if I have done wrong."

Reporters besieged the jurors, who were largely willing to talk. "I voted for the prisoner's conviction from the first to the last, and I think, of course, that I did right," said Oliver Briggs. Bram "was quick-witted enough on the stand, but I let my reasons guide me, not my sympathy, and I think we arrived at the reasonable verdict." Still, foreman Rinaldo Jack had to acknowledge, "We had good debaters on the jury, and we argued to discover a motive, but we couldn't find any." Incredibly, according to Harry Booth, he and three other jurors—Arnold, Dyer, and the God-fearing Howes—"voted against our convictions." The *Boston Post* started a solicitation for opinions—"Is the Bram Verdict Just?"—that ran for days and brought a heavy negative response.

Back in the marshal's office after the verdict, Bram received well-wishers who believed the verdict unjust. To a *Herald* reporter, Bram offered his thanks for fair treatment throughout from all of the press. "I am an innocent man, no matter what the verdict has been," he said. "Young man, when you are 20 or 30 years older, you can look back and say that you saw an innocent man found guilty of murder."

A guilty verdict was not generally expected. "A disagreement had been looked for," reported the *Sunday Herald* that afternoon. "The greatest anxiety was felt in many quarters lest the jury should fail to fix the crime upon the accused, and by this failure leave the question as to who committed the murders always open."

No one was more relieved by the verdict than the Monkses out in Brookline. "As for the members of the Monks family themselves, the great case in which Lester has figured so prominently has not been one which they cared to discuss with their friends and acquaintances. Much less do they care to express to reporters their opinions as to the result." The Monkses were content to exhale discreetly. Given what the family knew, their posture made eminent sense.

Yet Lester chose to entertain a reporter for the *Boston Morning Journal* at the family home, saying he appreciated the paper's "fair and conservative course" during the trial and that he would listen to any questions and choose whether to respond. "He was clad in a rich smoking gown, his small feet encased in velvet slippers, and between his lips was a dainty Turkish cigarette." The brief interview took place in the home's "sumptuously furnished parlor."

His opinion of the verdict? Though he had refused to answer that question from numerous other reporters, now "I will say that in my opinion the conviction was the natural outcome of the evidence against him. I consider the verdict a just one—one that was fully warranted by the evidence."

As to the discrepancy between his statements in Halifax and at trial: "Possibly there may have been slight discrepancies [but] upon our arrival in Halifax, my nerves were unstrung. I told the truth, the whole truth and nothing but the truth to the best of my recollection in both instances."

The theory of the crime he wrote up on board and everyone signed? "It was neither a theory or an agreement. Bram asked me to write up an account of the occurrences and I did so."

Any doubt that Brown actually saw from his position at the wheel all that he testified to? "Not the slightest."

Did Brown have any guilty knowledge of or was he a participant in the killings? "That is hardly a fair question. . . . I do not care to answer it in the affirmative or negative." There the interview ended, with that odd response.

Monks may have felt that Bram's conviction "was fully warranted by the evidence," but many others were not so sure. Weeks later, "it is generally conceded that the verdict of the jury does not by any means clear up the mystery surrounding the case." The *Albany Law Journal*, hardly a panting daily, noted that "while Bram may be the man who committed the three murders, the evidence of his guilt is far from satisfactory, and the question may still be asked: Who committed the murders for which Bram has been convicted? The case shows that in real life may occur mysteries deeper and more difficult of solution than any which the fertile imagination of the romancer is able to invent."

As far as Lester Monks was concerned, the case was closed. By late February, the *Boston Post* reported that Monks was settled at home in Brookline: "He sleeps well and he eats well and he seemingly enjoys life. He has no interest now in his former companions on board the Herbert Fuller."

"No," said Monks in brief comments, "I have not been down to the jail to see them, and I do not know how they are getting along, whether they are contented or not."

<hr />

IN MARCH, THE only sentence available for a guilty verdict in a federal murder case at the time of his trial was pronounced on Bram: death by hanging, scheduled for June. "In the presence of Almighty God," said Bram after Judge Colt condemned him, "I am innocent of the crime of which I am charged. God knows it, and will protect me." His lawyers, equally certain of his innocence, were aiming for more secular protection, from the US Supreme Court, the only appellate option after a federal circuit court verdict.

Two weeks after Bram was sentenced, his appeal was filed. On June 11, a week before his scheduled execution, he was summoned to court in Boston and told a stay had been granted until the Supreme Court ruled, which was expected during its October term.

The brief by French and Cotter alleged some sixty-seven errors by the trial court. It was a standard approach: throw things up and see what sticks. The hearing before the Court was in October; the decision came in mid-December. The narrow majority opinion— five to three (the ninth justice heard the arguments but retired two weeks before the decision)—was a minor landmark in Supreme Court jurisprudence.

It's often hard to predict what supposed errors an appellate court will focus on, but Justice Edward White, a Confederate Civil War veteran named to the court three years earlier, chose one that Bram's lawyers had not especially focused on: the interrogation by Halifax detective Nicholas Power of the chained and stripped Bram. White and the majority based their decision on the Fifth Amendment, the first time that amendment had featured prominently in a Supreme Court decision and the legal starting ground for the landmark *Miranda* decision seventy years later.

Earlier in 1896, White had sided with the overwhelming majority in the notorious *Plessy v. Ferguson* decision that upheld state segregation laws creating "separate but equal" public accommodations for blacks and whites. That southerner White might the same year author a decision to favor a black man was hardly to be expected. But his long court career often defied expectation; in 1910, he became the first sitting justice appointed chief justice.

"The rule is not," wrote White, "that in order to render a statement admissible the proof must be adequate to establish that the particular communications contained in a statement were voluntarily made, but it must be sufficient to establish that the making of the statement was voluntary; that is to say, that from the causes, which the law treats as legally sufficient to engender in the mind of the accused hope or fear in respect to the crime charged, the accused was not involuntarily impelled to make a statement, when but for the improper influences he would have remained silent."

By confronting Bram with Brown's supposed accusation, Detective Power produced upon Bram's "mind the fear that if he remained silent it would be considered an admission of guilt, and therefore render certain his being committed for trial as the guilty person."

The circumstances were also important: "Bram had been brought from confinement to the office of the detective, and there, when alone with him, in a foreign land, while he was in the act of being stripped or had been stripped of his clothing, was interrogated by the officer, who was thus, while putting the questions and receiving answers thereto, exercising complete authority and control over the person he was interrogating."

The standard, as White saw it, was that "in order to be admissible, [a confession] must be free and voluntary; that is, must not be extracted by any sort of threats or violence, nor obtained by any direct or implied promises, however slight, nor by the extension of any improper influence."

Justice White's majority included John Harlan (the lone dissenter in the notorious *Plessy* decision), George Shiras, Rufus Peckham, and Horace Gray. A few months earlier in the year, Justice Gray, a Boston-born graduate of Harvard and Harvard Law, had attended the wedding of Olga Gardner and George Monks, the uncle of Lester who, of course, was also present. Bram's stay of execution pending his Supreme Court appeal had been granted on June 11; the wedding, for which Gray and his wife returned to Boston, was four days later. Gray was well aware of Lester's involvement in the *Fuller* case, and Lester would have been well aware of Gray's pending involvement. It can't be known if the justice and the Harvard dropout spoke at the wedding, but the justice certainly showed the dropout no favor by voting to give Bram another chance.

Bram's conviction was reversed, and a new trial was ordered. Within hours, his lawyers, not yet having read the full text of the decision, were in Bram's cell to deliver the news. "I am glad, so glad," Bram said, "but you know I have felt all along that it would be this way. I thought the judges would see that I was an innocent man and would not let an innocent man be hanged. I am glad it has come out this way and that my hopes have been realized."

Of course, the decision was not all that Bram and lawyers might have hoped for. The decision was significant as a matter of constitutional law, but it didn't give Bram his freedom, just a second trial from which only his exchange with Nic Power in Halifax would be excluded.

Cotter and French were eager to defend Bram again, even if as court-appointed lawyers they were recovering only their costs and earning no fees. Sherman Hoar, meanwhile, had given up his US attorney position (to pursue business or political opportunities, briefly) and been replaced by Boyd Jones, an arch political and social conservative.

First trial juror Harry Booth was "glad that Bram was going to have a new trial." Fellow juror Abel Ford thought nothing had changed: "I do not believe any intelligent jury, unless prejudiced, will render a verdict different to the one rendered by the jury with whom I sat."

As it happened, a verdict different from what anyone at the first trial expected would be possible in the second trial. Less than two weeks after the verdict in the first trial, Congress created a new verdict in federal murder (and rape) cases: guilty, without capital punishment. When such a verdict was returned, the guilty person "shall be sentenced to imprisonment at hard labor for life."

While this new option may seem now like a softening of the penalty for murder, it was intended as a remedy for dramatically diminishing conviction rates in federal murder trials through the 1800s, to less than 20 percent (and even lower in state courts). Unfortunately, it became a verdict that could be used as a juridical shrug: an unholy compromise for a divided jury. Juries that could not agree on guilt and execution now could find guilt and feel less guilt of their own. Today's prisons hold many victims of such cowardice.

THE SECOND TRIAL for the murder of Captain Nash started on March 16, 1898, and lasted for more than a month, substantially longer than the first trial. The day before the jury got the case on April 20, the United States declared war on Spain. While interest in the trial in Boston was high—"More than 1000 people crowded the corridors of the federal building and . . . outside to get a glimpse of the famous prisoner" at the end of the first day—the nation's eyes had shifted to events in Cuba.

There were more witnesses, but the testimony of the main prosecution witnesses was largely similar to the first time around. Unfortunately, the fifth volume of the 1898 trial transcript, starting with page 3242—the first trial took up 2,200 pages in three volumes—comprising Bram's testimony and most of the defense case plus the closing arguments, is missing. Newspaper reporting provides only an editorial version of what was actually said.

The jury again was twelve white men, from a twenty-eight-year-old teacher to a sixty-two-year-old retired leather dealer; again, they were sequestered at a hotel (Young's) near the federal courthouse.

Monks this time testified for parts of three days, from the afternoon of the twenty-second through the morning of the twenty-fourth, roughly twice as long as during the first trial. He started truthfully, saying that he "had just left college" in June 1896 and that he was now a clerk in his father's office. He added "crackers, canned goods, and a box of oranges" plus "two or three hundred cigars" to his previously acknowledged inventory of alcohol. He testified that the axe in the storage room was generally visible because the door was propped open with a barrel.

Of relations between various people on board before the killings, Monks testified that his with Bram were "very pleasant"; between Bram and Nash, "very pleasant. The captain didn't have very much to say to him but, as far as he did, I failed to see any misunderstanding between them"; between Bram and Mrs. Nash, "very slight indeed." At the dinner table, she and Bram conversed "very little," she and Monks "a good deal," Nash and Bram "not much," and Nash and Monks "quite a little."

In all of the important substance, Monks's testimony was mostly the same as at the first trial, but there were some differences. Asked by the prosecutor what moisture he felt on his hand after placing it on the captain's shoulder, Monks said, "I don't know." When asked if afterward he discovered whether it was blood, Monks said, inexplicably, "I did not. I didn't notice any blood on my hand." At the first trial, he had, equally inexplicably, testified that he discovered the moisture was blood only a day later when the crew told him so.

As to the location of the axe when, again according to Monks, Bram spotted it jammed in the deck load, Monks placed it "just about forward of the forward companionway of the after house . . . a little to the port of the mizzenmast, about ten feet straight ahead forward of the companionway." This puts the axe a bit closer to the companionway than appeared in the first trial, an easier placement for whoever emerged from the cabin to put it there.

Curiously, Monks then testified that he was unsure who picked up the axe, either Spencer or Bram; at the first trial, it was uncontested that Spencer had done so. Then Monks added a new axe: "it was rather a light axe and what was known as the cabin axe, that is to say, it was very little used." Nothing further was asked about this second axe.

There was other new and unquestioned testimony by Monks. He said that after trying Bram's revolver with the old cartridges, Spencer "got disgusted and threw it overboard." There is no prior testimony that that happened.

On cross-examination by Cotter, Monks clarified that the sixty bottles of "very good beer" he brought were pints, not quarts, that in fact his father had bought them, and that Monks had been at them: "I drank quite a number of bottles." At the first trial, he said he had drunk very few.

Monks also clarified why he wanted the discovery of the captain's revolver under his mattress kept quiet. "I wasn't sure but the crew would rush out yet, and I thought if there was one more revolver they didn't have it would be a mighty good thing." That was the "sole reason" for his interest in not telling the crew. Monks added that the revolver was found under the middle of the mattress and that the mattress was three inches thick. Cotter did not ask how Monks had not noticed a bulky weapon—its cylinder nearly as thick as the mattress itself—for two weeks.

Cotter did ask again about Monks's encounter with the dying captain. Monks testified the captain's feet were just "three or four feet" away from Monks's door. When Monks put his hand on the captain's shoulder "to arouse him," Monks now said there was enough light to see the captain—"I did"—but not his wounds: "I didn't notice them . . . because there was not enough light to see his wounds, I suppose—I suppose that is the reason."

Some further inquiry about how Monks could see the captain well enough to feel his shoulder (and come away with what Monks said later he discovered to be blood) but not see his axe-battered face and head would seem to have been in order at that point, but Judge Colt called for a recess and Cotter didn't return to that line of questioning. Cotter did continue questioning Monks, at length, never catching him in a dramatic lie, but pecking away, as at a scab so that the wound might with time become infected.

In his closing argument, which we have only from a newspaper account, prosecutor Jones felt it necessary to bolster Monks's image: "Monks, honest boy, no matter what they may say about him—and there has been an attempt made to morally assassinate him—Monks says he saw that axe in the storeroom. He was not afraid to admit it, because he had no guilt on his soul." Jones returned to the maligned witness later: "Monks is a young man of 20 or 21 years, starting on the journey of life, which many of us have gone along a considerable distance, and the horrible cloud of suspicion which has been raised in the minds of people and in newspapers and elsewhere on the head of Lester H. Monks is one of those things which are hard to bear, but he is bearing it like a man."

Though it seemed like it at the time to many observers, Monks was not on trial, Bram was, and the jury dealt with him the next night, just after ten o'clock, following deliberations of less than eleven hours. This trial had been nearly twice as long as the first one; this jury was out less than half as long as the first one. Judge Colt's charge to this jury had been "exceedingly brief," only forty minutes; Judge Webb's to the first jury had taken nearly three times as long. Clearly, judges and jury had had enough.

———◆———

"GUILTY, BUT WITHOUT capital punishment," said the jury, one of the first juries to make use of the new option. In their deliberations, it soon emerged, the jurymen had voted fourteen times, at one time eleven to one, at another eight to four, for death. When it appeared the twelve jurors could not agree unanimously, at nine to three for death on the thirteenth ballot, they chose the new option: "The verdict was the result of a compromise," precisely what the new federal verdict option was not supposed to be. Strangely, or not, the first jury also, before its unanimous vote, had split nine to three.

The verdict was a "cowardly compromise in a capital case, and a sad commentary on trial by jury," said Cotter and French. "If the defendant committed the crime he should be hanged; if he is innocent, then it is a wicked act to condemn him to imprisonment."

Bram, looking "surprised by the verdict," shook his head with his face buried in his handkerchief, "as though mentally protesting against the verdict." Made available to reporters, Bram was uncharacteristically reticent: "I shall say nothing."

Few of the jurors spoke, but one, unnamed, provided deep insight: "We threw out the evidence of Charles Brown entirely. We did not take any stock in his statement that he could see into the cabin from the wheel with both hands on the wheel. We based our verdict on the circumstantial evidence entirely."

That the jury disregarded Brown entirely was wise; that they voted to send Bram to prison for life on thin and disputed circumstantial evidence seems a crime in itself.

Bram remained in the city jail while he and his lawyers considered whether to pursue another appeal. After several months, they decided to cut their losses. On the afternoon of July 12, 1898, exactly two years less a few hours and a day from the *Herbert Fuller* murders, Bram, with Cotter and French, appeared before Judge Colt and spoke before the mandatory sentence was pronounced.

"I can only refresh your honor's memory," Bram said, nervous at first, "of the undying fact that I am innocent of the crime with which I am charged. Injustice has been done to me. I am a victim of circumstances. All I have to say is to thank my counsel for the noble fight they have made for me. All I can say is to renew what I have always told them, that I am innocent. And may God bless them and all that have injured me." Without comment, Judge Colt then sentenced Bram to life in the nearby state prison at Charlestown.

Bram's offering of blessing on those who had injured him was readily learned by the remainder of the *Fuller*'s crew: they remained held, for a dollar a day with room and board, for many more months while US attorney Jones considered at his leisure whether to try Bram for the murders of Blomberg and Mrs. Nash. Oscar Anderson would be released first on bail, then Wassen, and finally, Loheac, Slice, Perdok, and Brown, in October 1899, when nearly everyone had forgotten about them. By then, Bram was well settled in prison.

And Lester Monks was busy constructing one of his own.

7

A MOST
UNFORTUNATE ENDING

I guess I'm down-and-out for all time.
—LESTER MONKS, APRIL 4, 1912,
IN "LETTERS OF A DOWN-AND-OUT,"
ATLANTIC MONTHLY, FEBRUARY 1913

Oliver Briggs was troubled about something. The Cambridge builder had been a leading and vocal proponent of Bram's guilt as a juror at the first trial. On the morning of April 18, 1900, a Wednesday, his wife rose early, leaving him alone in their bedroom. The older of their two sons, eighteen, had come in to talk with his father briefly and left the room. Just before seven, Briggs sat at the foot of his bed and raised a pistol to his head. "The bullet entered above the right eye and went completely through the skull." Death was immediate. Briggs was a popular figure in Cambridge, known as "a whole-souled, big-hearted man." He was forty-one and left his wife and three children. Business reverses were the rumored cause, but the truth was anyone's guess. Obituaries mentioned that he had been a Thomas Bram juror but not that he had been assertive about Bram's guilt.

After the trials, Lester Monks was a changed man. He might have returned to Harvard, where his younger brother, Archibald, intending to become a building engineer, started in 1899. Instead, Lester opted to leave youth behind and embark on life as a working adult, as his father had done.

At first he stayed close to home, working as a local salesman for the Morrisdale Coal Company, and kept his head down, refusing to answer the questions of reporters gathered outside his parents' house in July 1898 on the second anniversary of the *Fuller* murders. Late the following summer he ventured up to Cazenovia Lake, the guest again of his Harvard friend Dennis Emory.

Monks had first met Frances Frederica Leech at Cazenovia a few years earlier. By the summer of 1899, Frederica was a popular beauty. She was the daughter of John Frederick Leech and the former Margaretta Park, a prominent Washington couple whose American forebears had prospered in western Pennsylvania. Like Lester, Frederica's father was a noted golfer, a recent captain of the Chevy Chase Golf Club team. Frederica had made her society debut two seasons earlier; she was said to be "the most beautiful blonde in Washington society." Her parents were quite pleased on the last Sunday of the summer of 1899 to announce her engagement to Lester Monks, with a wedding planned for the following spring. Sadly, Dennis Emory would not be attending. He married in the fall of 1899 and four months later died of typhoid fever in Syracuse, his hometown.

Most of the many social announcements in the newspapers mentioned Lester's heroic role in the *Herbert Fuller* affair. Most also referred to his academic status, either with delicacy as having been a member of Harvard's class of '98, which was true, or falsely as having graduated with his class. No corrections were printed. As far as anyone outside friends and family knew, Lester was a Harvard man and there was no reason to upset perceptions.

In early November, Lester won the weekend's final club golf tournament of the local season, and Boston social columns listed him prominently among the theatergoers to *Lord and Lady Algy*, a popular, forgettable comedy. It seemed that Lester Monks, the alcoholic Harvard dropout who shipped on an axe-murder voyage, was launching into a proper society life.

In mid-April 1900, wedding invitations were sent, the "extremely pretty and graceful blonde" and Monks to be joined on May 10 at the Church of the Covenant in Washington. The *Boston Home Journal*, a cheeky society weekly, reported the planned wedding "in which Boston feels interest" between DC maiden Frederica and hometown's Lester Monks, "the well-known golfist." Close readers of the *Journal* might have picked up a scent that Lester was not quite up to par.

In May, they married, a headlining "Brilliant Wedding" of a society couple. "Mrs. Monks is the granddaughter of David Wells, a multi-millionaire of Pittsburg. Mr. Monks belongs to the well-known Massachusetts family of that name and is a recent graduate of Harvard." His intimates must have marveled at his good fortune: a beautiful bride and a Harvard degree. Among the many notable wedding guests were New York governor Theodore Roosevelt and his wife, Edith.

A month later Roosevelt would be the Republican nominee for vice president and, the following year, president after McKinley's assassination. As president, Roosevelt would make Asa French the US attorney for Boston. Later, influenced by his friend Mary Rinehart's belief in Thomas Bram's innocence, Roosevelt would urge Woodrow Wilson to pardon Bram. Roosevelt's opinion of Monks is unrecorded.

Lester and Frederica settled in Brookline. For a while, all was well. Monks continued at Morrisdale Coal for two years until he and George Eddy Warren, a manager at Morrisdale Coal and a family friend—he had been an usher at Lester's wedding—in

January 1903 formed Warren & Monks, engaged in coastal shipping of coal. Warren was president and Monks treasurer.

Warren, from an old New England family, was eight years older
than Lester. He had grown up in Newton, outside Boston, and graduated from Brown. The company was headquartered at 35 Congress
Street, the Monks family building in Boston, with an office in New
York City. Initially, Warren & Monks was the New England agent
for the New River Consolidated Coal & Coke Company, a large
producer based in West Virginia. The business soon broadened.

A long item in a mining-industry magazine in February 1904
reported that Warren & Monks was "to be congratulated on having secured so large and fine a list of coals to handle." Brief biog-
raphies of the principals included the by then routine assertion
that Monks "is a graduate of Harvard."

By July, Warren & Monks, having acquired other coal shippers, had become "one of the most important coal combines in
the East." That month, they purchased the Eastern Coal Company, of Providence, Rhode Island, itself a recent consolidation of
three smaller coal companies, for a substantial half-million dollars. "The deal is of importance" because it gave Warren & Monks
"increased facilities and a wider outlet for their coal in New England territory."

In due course, Eastern Coal's treasurer was replaced by Monks,
now described as "a prominent coal man of Boston." By the end of
1904, Warren & Monks had set up a branch office in New Haven,
"for the purpose of facilitating and handling of its large business
in that territory." In the several years ahead, the company reported
good business handling coal shipments from Newport News, Virginia, and other eastern ports. In 1907, the company opened an
office in Newport News, then a booming coal port. Lester seemed
to be succeeding in business.

Yet he couldn't help himself on occasion from returning to
the subject of the *Fuller* and Thomas Bram. In March 1903, while

in Worcester arranging coal sales, Monks told a reporter for the *Worcester Telegram* that Bram had offered $10,000 to the first mate of the *White Wings* to poison the captain. Monks also described Bram as "a surly fellow, uncommunicative and disagreeable, and not a good sailor," and he claimed that Bram had confessed to the *Fuller* murders to an official in Halifax. There is no evidence for any of Monks's claims. What prompted them mystified Bram's former lawyer. "I don't know what Mr. Monks intended by that," James Cotter told the *Boston Morning Journal* the next day; he labeled Monks's various assertions a "yarn" and "absurd." For whatever reason, Monks seemed still to be contemplating his past.

Meanwhile, he was pursuing life with and without Frederica. She was often away from Boston. In March 1901, she spent three weeks with her parents in Washington, where she "extensively entertained." Such visits gradually increased, while another number stayed at zero: children, what every proper wife was expected then to provide for her husband. In the spring of 1904, Frederica was again in Washington, having "temporarily deserted her beautiful estate in Brookline," as well as her husband. It was not reported whether she was with Lester in Belgrade, Maine, that May when he landed a "beautiful specimen," a seven-pound lake trout.

Business did not keep Lester from fishing; for several weeks in July 1905, he was up in Maine, catching bass on the fly. Back in January, leaving her husband to his work, Frederica spent some weeks in Washington with her sister, Marian, who had married a few years earlier. The society pages had noted then that Mrs. Monks was "a very charming society woman."

Lester presumably left Frederica for his July 1905 fishing trip aware that he had impregnated her. On January 13, 1906, after six years of marriage, Frederica gave birth to David Park Monks; he would prove to be their only son. Two Augusts later came a daughter, Frederica, born in Newport, during her parents' summer residence at a Leech family seaside cottage in nearby Jamestown.

For unknown reasons, the Monks family of four unseasonably remained in Jamestown well into October before returning home to Brookline.

Perhaps Lester's taste for extended time away from the office had something to do with the breakup of Warren & Monks in the following spring of 1908, when the older partner established the George E. Warren Company. Warren soon transitioned from coal to petroleum, and his business expanded. He died in 1935, leaving a wife and no children. The company thrives today as an international energy distribution company, out of Florida, still saluting its founder by motto: "By barge, by pipeline, by tank truck, by George."

Lester made a go at business on his own. In 1908, he established the Monks Coal Company, with himself as president and treasurer, at a comfortable salary of $5,475 (roughly $1 million in economic status today).

It appears that in the split of Warren and Monks, the latter got the office at the family building and the former got the clients. In exchange for paying himself well, Lester worked little, while the company worked hard at racking up debts. By October 1909, Monks Coal was in receivership, and the receiver went to court to recover Monks's salary, for which he had rendered no "adequate service," plus another $9,000 that he owed the company. The receiver asked that interest Monks was receiving under his grandfather's will be taken to cover his company debts.

In its reporting on the collapse of Monks Coal, the *Boston Post* had nothing to say about its namesake's past decade of business life; instead, he was identified only as the passenger aboard the *Herbert Fuller*, with recaps of its murderous voyage and the legal aftermath. Lester might well have felt his past catching up to him: he was not a currently notable coal businessman of the new century; he was a former notable player in an old notorious crime.

The following March, as might be expected, Frederica left him. She took the two children with her back to Washington. For "a long and continuous period of time," as it turned out, she had been subjected to abuse by Lester. In the language of the divorce papers, it was "cruel and abusive treatment," in Brookline and Boston, causing "serious injury to her health, rendering it necessary for her to leave [home] and seek protection elsewhere."

Today, cruel and abusive treatment is the most common fault-based grounds for divorce in Massachusetts; actual physical abuse is generally needed beyond mental cruelty. A century ago, fewer than one in five Massachusetts divorces were for cruel and abusive treatment, trailing desertion and adultery. In 1911, in Norfolk County—when and where Frederica's divorce was granted—there were 110 divorces, only 30 on her grounds. For marriages of ten to twenty years, as was hers, her divorce was one of only 4. Which perhaps made the hurt more acute.

At the brief divorce proceedings in Norfolk County Court in September 1911, only Frederica and her doctor testified. Lester did not contest the divorce, and it was promptly granted. Sole custody of the children was given to Frederica; Lester and his parents were permitted to see the children at times to be determined. Those times turned out to be very few.

As with his recent business failure, the several newspaper accounts of his marital failure made no mention of Lester's business career; all recalled only his role in the *Herbert Fuller* affair fifteen years earlier. "Divorce Defendant Prominent in Mate Bram Trial," proclaimed the *Boston Post*, as if the one event naturally sprang from the other, which as a continuum of violence it might have. In December, a *Post* social column noted "quite a succession of Boston men to select Washington girls for their brides" in recent years. Last in the long list was Lester Monks, whose marriage to Frederica Leech "has had a most unfortunate ending."

Frederica would soon remarry, by all accounts happily. Lester, though, was lost, and, for a second time, his family sent him away. Sixteen years earlier, he was a Harvard dropout put aboard a ship to clear his head and liver. Now he was thirty-five years old, with a decade of marriage, family, and business, and nothing to show for any of it. His parents' "patience finally came to an end," his younger cousin wrote; "they provided him with a one-way ticket and in effect told him to 'get lost.'"

The ticket was aboard a ship to Seattle, then a grubby and over-grown post-Alaska gold-rush town. Its population had doubled to eighty thousand during the 1890s and tripled again during the next decade, but the growth had (and has) been relatively stagnant since. It was a suitable way station for the wrecked life of Lester Monks, who observed that he "landed in Seattle with three dollars and a half, thoroughly dirty, and without any baggage except a tin box of cigarettes." He was a remittance man, without remittance: no family money was awaiting him in Seattle.

For a week in early March 1912, Monks lived in a Turkish bath in the basement of a cheap hotel, selling off his shirt studs and cuff buttons for food money and making use of the bath's amenities to wash and dry his one set of clothes. "I never before wore one shirt for so many days, but as I didn't have any money I could not buy another," he wrote in the first of many letters to a friend in Boston. He attempted to find a proper job in the coal business or something related, but no one would have him. "I presume my appearance was somewhat against me as my suit of clothes looked pretty tough."

He worked one night as a stevedore and served as second for one bout of a prizefighter, who was rubbed down at the bath. Then with a rich fellow he met—a man named Jones who had four dollars—they moved into "a dump called the Hotel Rainer, one of those places that have (to me) the most disagreeable smell in the world: that of poverty." Their room was 75 cents a day, and Lester could not afford his share. "So, in desperation," they moved on to Cosmopolis, on a coastal bay a hundred miles southwest of Seat-tle, to work in a lumber mill. Arriving at night, they briefly found rest in a boardinghouse, until bedbugs chased them to the ground

outdoors. It was a strange life to which Monks had descended—
the prince turned pauper—but he seemed to relish cleansing himself in the gutter.

He and Jones lasted three ten-hour days at the mill, acquiring
splinters, aching backs, and a couple of dollars, before the foreman
pressed them into service fighting Wobblies mustered outside the
mill, protesting the $26 monthly wage less numerous deductions.
The subforeman "made a beautiful tackle on the extreme end of
the enemy's line and I followed suit. My I.W.W.'s head struck the
inside rail and after he hit he lay still." Still and presumably not
dead, before someone else "hopped up and tried to kick me in the
head; this made me sore, so, arising, I biffed a man in the left eye
and he my right."

After the union army retreated, the sheriff arrived, offering
Monks and Jones $5 a day to act as guards, which they did for a
week before tensions eased and Monks decided he agreed with the
strikers. He and Jones quit and headed north eight hundred miles
by steamer to Prince Rupert, British Columbia. Seattle steamship
agents had promised that jobs would materialize there within five
minutes off the boat.

It was snowing hard when they landed on April 3. "I had walked
the streets of Cosmopolis so vigorously that I wore a hole completely through my right shoe and the snow was wet." He walked
the wet streets of Prince Rupert looking for a job at offices, stores,
and docks and came up empty, as did Jones. After finding shelter
for the night and no food for more than a day, and with a penny
between them, Monks "walked up to a perfect stranger and said,
'Give me a dollar.' (I didn't say, I want to borrow, but Give.) He
gave." This provided a drink apiece, 25 cents worth of food, and a
remaining 10 cents for coffee and doughnuts. "I guess I'm down-
and-out for all time. I'm a sight, trousers torn and a week or ten
days of beard which, I regret to say, is turning quite gray, giving me
the appearance of a venerable old bum."

The following midnight, Monks and Jones got work shoveling coal—hot coal—from the hold of a newly arrived ship. In an hour, Jones passed out, overwhelmed by coal gas; Monks hung on until the job was complete at midmorning and then "fainted and fell flat on my face in the snow." That afternoon they collected their pay—35 cents for Jones, $3.25 for Monks—and they splurged on steak and coffee for $1.10. The next day, Monks's fortunes turned: a promise of work sixty miles inland building a steel bridge with concrete piers over the Skeena River for the Grand Trunk Pacific Railway: $3.00 a day less 90 cents for meals and $2.00 a month for doctor and hospital care. Parting with Jones, Monks became one of two hundred members of a pick-and-shovel gang, housed forty to a bunkhouse, with straw mattresses and no bedbugs.

The setting inspired Monks. Bold mountains and the Skeena— "the second perfect-looking fly-fishing stream" (the other in Maine)—that he hoped to test when warming weather melted the heavy snow. The ten-hour workdays weren't especially hard and quickly proved "fearfully monotonous," but there were risks. One morning in mid-April, a tether on a wooden derrick parted, and Monks and two other workers were sent climbing out to the end, forty feet high, to attach a new line. The derrick's arm collapsed. "When I felt the timbers going I jumped outwards and landed in the river, reaching shore some two hundred yards downstream in an eddy." He was the lucky one. "Both my companions were killed, one instantly, the other dying in about an hour. The bodies are lying at my feet, covered up with some meal-sacks. A good horse is worth $500, but a man nothing, in this country."

This prompted reflection. In a few days, "I will be thirty-six years old, working with my hands, with no prospect of improving my condition." All around him were fish "in almost inconceivable numbers, also great mineral wealth and much timber; but all this is for the capitalist and not for the working-man."

By early May, Monks had acquired a few clothes items, dearly bought from the company story. One day he discovered that one of his two flannel shirts had disappeared. "If I could get my hands on the man that stole it there would be a near murder." Meanwhile, lice and fleas found their way into the bunkhouse. Monks asked his superintendent for lumber to build his own shack. "'Stay in the bunk-house or get out'; so I got."

He hiked four hours upriver to Seeley, the end of navigation on the Skeena, consisting of eleven board buildings and twice as many tents, and then two more hours on to New Hazelton, with sixty frame buildings and tents in equal numbers plus a log-cabin branch of the Union Bank of Canada. The date was May 7. Exactly twelve years earlier, he had left Boston for Washington to get married. "My prospects at that time seemed to be bright and secure, but as the late lamented [comedian] Dan Daly used to say, 'Now look at the damn thing.'" But the local contractor for the railway was there, and the next day Monks had a job: timekeeper/shopkeeper of Camp 26A, a four-hour hike up a branch of the Skeena to where the longest tunnel on the railroad was being dug.

Camp 26A had only fifty men, engaged in cut-and-cover work. The outgoing timekeeper briefed Monks briefly and left. He discovered that the camp coffee was the best he'd had since New York and that the camp cook did well enough with beef, potatoes, and tea three times a day. Monks's first day in camp would have been his twelfth anniversary, had he still been married. Two days later, he got his hair cut for the first time in two months, by the camp blacksmith: "It's getting pretty gray, and my eyesight is not what it was."

In other regards, Monks experienced a rebirth. For the camp store, he built shelves; for himself, a chair, the "first armchair I've sat in for seven weeks." He fashioned a rake to collect camp garbage that he then burned. In the back of his store with auger and saw he cut a window for badly needed light and ventilation and in the front fashioned a self-closing screen door, providing a refuge from black flies and especially mosquitoes: "I would swear some of them have an over-all spread of wings of at least an inch and a half." He mended the cook's assembling table and cut a hinged skylight to ventilate the cookhouse. To avoid drinking water from a small stream out of a swamp "full of wrigglers," he dug a well, a "great improvement over the present water-supply." Reviving a passion, he fashioned a fishing rod and on nearby streams started catching landlocked salmon.

He had many moments to consider his fate. Since March 1910—over two years—he had seen his children once: "I wonder when I'll see them again. In a year or never." He seemed resigned to his new life. "It would rather seem as though from here out my life would be passive and rather in the rôle of spectator. . . . I went at a fast and furious pace from 1898 to 1912. What a lot of work I did crowd in during those years! The [deleted] king of New England seemed to be in sight, and now I'm a petty clerk in the wilds of British Columbia. Truly, it's a funny old world, but as a rule the sporting expression, 'They never come back,' I fancy, is a true one. I don't suppose I ever will."

Monks very quickly exhausted intellectual companionship with his camp mates. "I wish I had a dog," he wrote in mid-May; a week later, the timekeeper at a nearby camp gave him one, the puppy offspring of fox and Irish terriers. Formally named Tony Christo del Monte Monks, he helped his master "pass some idle moments." The relationship started thoughts of rekindling the life to which he'd been accustomed. "I don't dare to return either to semi- or full civilization without a job in sight or some money. . . . If I had a few dollars I believe I would try it, but, of course, it's out of the question to-day, and yet as this job will be (for me) through by October 1st at the latest . . . I may be driven to it." His prospects were slim. "I fully realize that a man going on to thirty-seven should be at about his best, and if I either had ability, or have any left, it is being wasted here in the woods; but, having studied the situation from every angle, I can't see any way out. I don't want to go hungry again and to be frank I'm afraid to tackle town-life again without either the above-mentioned job or money to get along on until something turns up."

By late August, his pay had risen to seventy-five dollars a month, leading to further thoughts of his recent life and its possible improvement. "My life for fifteen years or thereabouts has been very much out of the ordinary. . . . Of late I have wondered just how 'cracked' I am. Presume more rather than less, but . . . I've been through some pretty tough experiences and they have left marks and effects. . . . It does seem an awful waste to lead the life I am leading now, if I have it left in me to do things again. . . . It's rather hard not to ever see one's son and little daughter and to be completely cut off from every one you know."

In late September, a dog from a nearby camp, "a most interesting beast," adopted Monks. From Pete Seymour, a local Indian, Monks learned Jerry's history. Two falls earlier, Pete had tied the dog's future mother to a tree in the woods. As expected, timber wolves found her and when they were done "paying their respects," Pete shot them before they would kill her. The offspring, Jerry, now eighteen months old, 150 pounds, and more like a wolf than a dog, was "the queerest combination of bravery and timidity possible. . . . He will tackle a bear in a minute, but if something drops behind him he will put his tail between his legs and run like the veriest cur." He looked like a wolf but rested his head in Monks's lap. He would play with Monks but only if no one else was in sight. His sound was neither dog's bark nor wolf's howl. "His sleep is most incredibly light, a field-mouse will bring him to his feet in a second and, unlike a dog, when on his feet, he is wide awake." During the previous week, a pack of wolves were around the camp, and Jerry spent several nights with them. "Their nightly howling is evidently too much for him to stand. Apparently he wants to get out with the bunch."

So did his master. "The steel is only thirteen miles below us now and, when the wind is fair, we can hear the locomotive. This I rather resent, as it means civilization and that is something which, without clothes and position, I positively dread." But these were things he resolved once again to obtain.

Lester's musings in the Pacific Northwest were in the form of letters to an unnamed friend back in Boston, a former Harvard classmate. Lester's literate and emotional letters prompted the friend to offer them in a packet to another Harvard friend of his, Ellery Sedgwick, class of 1894, who had recently acquired the venerable but fading *Atlantic Monthly*. Sedgwick would run the magazine for three decades, restoring it to a prominence it retains. Before sending the letters to Sedgwick, the friend thoroughly blacked out the writer's signature on each, substituting the initials "H. D. P." But some biographical information was provided, as indicated by the editorial note introducing "Letters of a Down-and-Out" in the *Atlantic's* February 1913 issue:

> The author is a young man who, soon after leaving Harvard College, started life with excellent prospects, and early in his career achieved marked material success. While still in the earliest thirties, he was making an income of $25,000 a year in a wholesale commission business; he was married, apparently happy, the father of two children, and, in the current phrase, "fixed for life." Then misfortune came. He lost his position and his money, and at thirty-five, stripped of everything he possessed, he went, without money, friends, or references, to try a new start in the West. The following letters, practically unchanged except for the alteration and omission of names, take up his story at this point.

This brief and not fully accurate profile offered no reason for the advent of his misfortune. The *Atlantic* published a large selection of the letters, in the February and March issues. It should have been easy for Boston contemporaries to figure out the letter writer's identity from the information in the editorial note, plus public knowledge of Monks's divorce and disappearance from Boston and a copy of the Harvard Class of 1898 Quindecennial Report of 1913. That report noted that Monks's biographical entry was repeated from the previous class report, of 1904, that his address was "unknown" and his status "Lost." And there is Lester's first dog, Tony Christo del Monte Monks, whose last name, under the guidelines announced in the *Atlantic*'s editorial note, should have been omitted.

A postscript note after the concluding letter in the March issue indicated that the *Atlantic* "has no further information concerning the writer of these letters beyond the bare fact that he has acquired a steady position." How the *Atlantic* knew that and all the information in the introductory note is unclear. Editor and publisher Sedgwick was nobody's fool, and he knew just about everybody it was necessary to know in Boston and everything about them. Indeed, a "long known" friend of Sedgwick's was Lester's "kindly, warmhearted" uncle George, who certainly knew of Lester's situation.

If it was the mutual friend of Monks and Sedgwick who provided the letters changing only their signature, then it was Sedgwick who did the alteration and omission of names of familiar Boston people and places to further mask Monks's identity. In any case, in his memoirs many years later, Sedgwick claimed not to know the letters' author, until Monks identified himself to him.

Before that, Monks was publicly identified. The "scion of one of Boston's oldest and wealthiest families," exaggerated a newspaper in September, "is struggling to earn his daily bread as a common laborer somewhere in the Northwest." In quoting material from the *Atlantic* letters and ascribing them to Monks, the paper was apparently the first to put the clues together. Sedgwick apparently was unaware of the reporting.

"It must have been a full year later that I was excited by a call on the telephone," Sedgwick wrote in his memoirs; "H. D. P. was on the line." He revealed himself as Monks to Sedgwick and, over a three-hour lunch that day, sometime in the spring of 1914, told Sedgwick his story, more of it than he had told anyone else and much more than what was revealed at Bram's trials. Sedgwick wrote in his memoirs thirty years later:

> From earliest boyhood, Monks had made a specialty of excitement. His family was armored by every Bostonian convention, and to the polite social pressures of his environment he had reacted violently. Drink first diverted, then interested, then absorbed him, and I gathered that before he went to Harvard he was a veteran of the bottle. The Dean soon took notice and toward spring of Lester's freshman year his relation with the University terminated with abruptness. But this was not the worst phase of the matter. His nerves were gone, his digestion ruined, and the doctors reported that delirium tremens was not far off.

Sedgwick painted a largely accurate—the Harvard separation we know was toward the end of Lester's second year—if somewhat overdramatic portrait and went on to tell the tale of the *Herbert Fuller* murders, apparently as told to him by Monks.

Sedgwick's telling discords somewhat with the trial record. He writes that Monks found the captain "in a bath of blood" and saw Mrs. Nash "in her bunk and the blankets were dripping blood." Possibly Sedgwick dramatized what Monks told him, or perhaps Monks told Sedgwick more than he told two courtrooms two decades earlier.

Sedgwick believed that his publication of Monks's letters "did more to strengthen Lester's morale and interest him once again in human relationships than almost anything else." Reluctantly, Sedgwick never published in the *Atlantic* a story that he had engaged Lester to write: his story of the *Herbert Fuller*. It never ran, and Monks never wrote it because of his mother.

Mrs. Monks, "so fearful of her position and as distressed that her son's name should be again on men's tongues," came to Sedgwick's office "and begged me to refuse further contributions of Lester." Sedgwick "spoke very plainly all that I felt," but in the end Lester "refrained from [writing] out of regard for his mother's advice." And eventually, as Sedgwick admitted in 1946 to an admirer of his published memoirs, "on account of George Monks I said nothing about all of this in the book."

What Lester might have written about the *Herbert Fuller* could have set the story straight or confounded it for all time. Some years later, he wrote this in his Harvard class report: "From 1910 to 1915, I built railroads in the Canadian Northwest." Of course, it was for less than half that time, and Monks did not mean for his classmates to take him literally. But if that is how he chose to present his railroad labors—as a falsehood wrapped in an appearance of truth—it is just as well that he did not present his version of the *Fuller* voyage.

In truth, Monks returned east in 1914 to find that Frederica had remarried the previous September, "very quietly" in Washington, to Hugh Black Rowland, a "brilliant lawyer." Frederica's parents did not attend, reportedly due to her mother's illness. Frederica's mother did not recover; she died a year later. Other deaths followed. Lester and Frederica's young daughter, Frederica, died in June 1916 at a children's hospital in Washington, after a prolonged but unspecified illness. She was just nine. Seven months later, the elder Frederica herself died, at age thirty-eight, again of unspecified causes. From Lester's past life, only his son, David, survived, but he remained in Washington for the time being with his stepfather, who had become the boy's legal guardian.

Monks tried to fill in the blanks, in familiar ways. By April 1916, he had obtained a position with William H. Randall & Company, a shipping business that owned or operated a number of freight vessels sailing out of Boston. It also functioned as an employment agency of sorts for Harvard men. Two years earlier, Boston-born William "Harry" Randall, a Harvard student for one year, with Harris Livermore (Harvard, '00) and others had established the Shawmut Steamship Company, which owned or controlled a varying number of ships. After the war, Monks would become a Shawmut board member.

Shawmut, like Randall & Company, would have a dizzying corporate history, with Monks in varied executive positions at both and other related entities. While the companies' dealings were often front-page news, Lester's actual role was shrouded. A profile of the company's officers included Monks, "whose family has been in the shipping business for nearly three hundred years, first down on Cape Cod and later in Boston." Presumably, Lester himself created the fanciful family history.

In keeping with his new image, in January 1917, two weeks after his ex-wife's death, Lester bought a yacht. The eighty-one-foot flush-deck, gaff-rigged racing schooner *Valmore* was famously and formerly owned by William Hale Thompson, who campaigned it successfully on the Great Lakes before becoming the model of corruption as Chicago mayor "Big Bill" Thompson. Monks, accomplished sailor in his youth, anticipated racing the boat out of Marblehead. If he did, there is no record; his ownership was likely very brief, especially as his finances, regardless of his various corporate titles, were so thin that it seems unlikely he had the means to finance the purchase of the yacht, much less campaign it.

On Christmas night 1945, long after Monks's brief ownership, the aging *Valmore*, en route from New York to Florida with a crew of four—two men and two teens, including a father and son—sank in a frigid gale on Frying Pan Shoals off Cape Fear, North Carolina. After seventy-two hours, the four sailors, in the yacht's twelve-foot dory, washed up on Wrightsville Beach, suffering from exposure but alive. Said one, "It was only the work of God that we survived." The *Valmore* did not, though by then it had survived much longer than its onetime owner Monks.

If Lester's attempt to rekindle his affinity with sailboats was not demonstrably successful, he did quickly find himself a new wife. On June 5, 1917, just five months after the *Valmore* acquisition and his first wife's death, Monks married Caroline Townsend Coxe, a wealthy fixture in the New York City social register. Lester had met Frederica when they were both teens summering in upstate New York. How cash-strapped forty-year-old divorcé Lester met Caroline, twenty-six years old with no great beauty and diminishing prospects but plenty of old money, is unclear. They married, without bridesmaids or ushers, in a small church in the New York City suburb of Rye, followed by a reception for immediate family and intimate friends at the nearby home of the bride's aunt Mrs. Richard Wainwright; the imposing stone mansion on Rye's harbor survives as a holistic learning center and rental-event location.

The *Boston Sunday Herald* society page item announcing the wedding, likely submitted by the bride's parents, noted that Lester Hawthorne Monks was "Harvard, '98." There was no mention of Lester's lack of a degree, of the *Herbert Fuller*, or of the groom's marital, family, or business history and situation.

Under the influence of his new wife, who had money, as Lester did not, they took up residence in New York City, in a fine late-1850s Italianate townhouse at 18 West Ninth Street that the new Mrs. Monks bought in her own name. People seem not to stay long there, with a dozen or more owners over the years; Uma Thurman's five-year ownership in the early 2000s consisted mostly of a three-year renovation. In any case, when the Monkses lived there, Caroline was the owner, and she would sell more quickly than Uma.

Lester did not waste time making a new family. On April 2, just less than ten months after her wedding, Caroline gave birth to a daughter, also named Caroline, much as Lester's late daughter, Frederica, had been named after his late first wife, Frederica. Marriage and a child can be joyous affirmations in a life that has had trouble. It would be a challenge for Monks to make them so.

8

BRAM UNBOUND

The aim of my life is to find the guilty man.
—THOMAS BRAM, *BOSTON GLOBE*, AUGUST 28, 1913

While Lester Monks was gaining and losing wives, business, and social standing, Thomas Bram went to prison and was mostly forgotten—for a bit.

In July 1906 the number of life prisoners at the Charlestown prison topped eighty for the first time. The *Boston Herald* observed that "a man sentenced to confinement for life passes very quickly from the public notice; one by one they go over to Charlestown and there, are forgotten." For example, the paper noted, it was not many years earlier that Bram was convicted in the murders aboard the *Herbert Fuller* and "the columns of the newspapers were given over lavishly to the story of the deed and of the legal fight of the prisoner to secure his freedom." Now, just ten years after the killings, the average man remembered that they happened, "but, if you ask him for the details of the matter, he is somewhat uncertain. Perhaps he will say: 'Bram is serving a life sentence, is he not?'"

A few months later, Bram was still serving his life sentence, but not in Massachusetts. In November 1906, he was transferred from

Charlestown to the new and larger federal prison in Atlanta. Bram had grown attached to Charlestown warden H. F. Bridges, "a true and loyal friend," and resisted the move. "I have been here now more than eight years and during that time I have been treated with the utmost kindness and consideration." Tearfully expressing "an abiding faith that he would one day be vindicated," Bram said he had been satisfied at Charlestown, "as satisfied as any man can be who is serving a life sentence for a crime of which he is not guilty. Who knows what sort of treatment I will receive in the place to which they are sending me?"

As it happened, the Atlanta prison and its warden were even better for Bram. Drawing on his earlier experience in the restaurant business, he became a cook in the Atlanta penitentiary's kitchen, which made him a central character in the daily life of the place, much as Spencer had been aboard the *Herbert Fuller*.

By February 1911, Bram was preparing a pardon application, with an array of supporting documents and input from local legal professionals whom Bram had interested in his case. "I have reached the conclusion, after considerable investigation, that Bram is absolutely innocent," prominent Atlanta lawyer Daniel Rountree wrote to James Finch, who as the pardon attorney at the US Justice Department reviewed and made recommendations to the president on all pardon applications. "Indeed," Rountree asserted, "I believe him incapable of the atrocious crime of which he was convicted."

Submitting the formal pardon application to Finch a month later, Rountree wrote that Bram's conduct, kindness, subservience, and general demeanor had "convinced all of the officers of the prison that he is incapable of having committed the atrocious crime." Rountree asked Finch to solicit the views of the prison warden and others. It was an unusual request, but Finch agreed to it.

William H. Moyer, a generally well-regarded reformist career warden, was a Bram supporter. After knowing Bram for more than four years, warden Moyer wrote Finch that "all of his actions, his attitude, his apparent nature, his open face, and the total absence of those things which generally mark a cruel and brutal nature have convinced me that he is not now capable of committing such a horrible triple tragedy." Bram's "very nature is inconsistent with guilt. . . . I would not find it difficult to believe that he was erroneously convicted."

Others wrote similarly. The prison's chief cook under whom Bram worked considered him "a model prisoner [who] would demand a good salary as a cook if he had his freedom." Bram "will be a worthy citizen" if pardoned, something he deserved, "as I feel the man is innocent of the crime which he is accused of." A kitchen and dining room guard wrote that Bram had never violated a prison rule and was always respectful, truthful, and faithful: "His cheerfulness is an inspiration to many of the men around him and I believe his every deed is actuated by the highest motives. I cannot think such a man gulity [*sic*] of the crime with which he is charged." The prison physician, A. L. Fowler, had observed Bram for five years: "Bram is as tender as a woman when preparing food for a sick prisoner, and when the prisoner was unable to eat it, Bram would ask my permission to prepare some delicacy or daintier food to tempt the sick man's appetite. This has happened often." With the possible exception of one other prisoner (a man who killed his wife and, despite a commutation from President Taft, chose to remain the prison pharmacist), "Bram has been the most faithful, efficient, and attentive man ever connected with the [prison] Hospital." Dr. Fowler was certain that Bram "is innocent. Men of his kind do not commit atrocious murders."

Prison chaplain T. C. Tupper wrote that Bram's deportment "as a prisoner and a man . . . has been most exemplary." In his conduct with officials and prisoners, "every action has been the impulse of a sincere Christian character. In fact, his conduct all along has been very commendable." Finch also heard from the pastor of the First Baptist Church in Charlestown, who was close to Bram during his prison years there: "I think well of him and feel that there are strong reasons which should commend him to clemency. I sincerely hope that this effort in his behalf may be successful."

Atlanta prison steward and storekeeper Jonathan W. Boyle, in daily contact with Bram, was likewise impressed: "He has always been open, frank, straightforward, earnest, sincere, and truthful. In his work he is energetic, patient, painstaking, and I have never known him to neglect it in any way. . . . I have long believed this man innocent of the crime with which he is charged." Boyle noted that Bram's fifteen years in prison had not hardened him: "Bram has suffered much but he is generally cheerful, optimistic, hopeful, and best of all not embittered toward anyone. I believe this man is innocent, and that the vile wretch who laid three victims low in death, made yet another victim of Thos. Bram. I hope this man will be returned as soon as possible to liberty and the place among men to which his industry, his uprightness, his worth, and the nobility of his character of right entitle him."

And so, with these character references and many others, Bram's pardon petition went to Washington in March 1911, with the pointed assertion in his formal application that Bram was "absolutely innocent of the crime of which he was convicted upon the testimony of strongly prejudiced witnesses, one or more of whom testified against him in order to shield themselves." Those witnesses, Monks and Brown, remained unnamed in the pardon application. At that time, 1911, Brown had disappeared into a Swedish mental institution and Monks was being divorced by his first wife.

Pardon attorney Finch, with no deadline to act, continued to solicit and receive opinions on Bram. Essential to Bram's cause were his trial lawyers, with whom he remained in close contact. In early December 1911, Asa French wrote a long account to Finch of the essential facts in the sequence of events on the ship and at

Bram's trials. French, who by then was the US district attorney in Boston, spoke for himself and Cotter in telling Finch, "We have both always believed in Bram's innocence."

Belief in Bram's innocence was not shared by all. "The pardon of this man Bram would be a sensational outrage," Boyd Jones wrote to Attorney General George Wickersham in mid-December 1911. Bram's second prosecutor had served just four years as a district attorney before taking up private practice in Boston. He wrote Finch in February, "I have not entertained the slightest doubt of his guilt and have been unable to see how any person could arrive at any other conclusion."

Jones was a person of slight doubt. He would go on to cofound the Sentinels of the Republic, a reactionary right-wing, antilabor group supported by various members of the Du Pont family and other prominent industrialists. The Sentinels flourished through the 1920s and '30s and folded amid world war in 1944 when its funds were donated to Williams College to endow an annual prize for student research in American politics. The liberality of each year's winners possibly torments Jones's soul.

Judge Webb had died in 1902, but LeBaron Colt was still alive in 1912 and felt compelled to offer his opinion: "I cannot conscientiously say that I have any doubt that the jury rendered a proper and just verdict in both the Bram trials."

Prominent Bostonians not directly connected to the case also weighed in. Notable among them was Ezra Ripley Thayer, a graduate of Harvard College (1888) and Harvard Law (1891) who had become dean of the law school in 1910. Thayer, "a man of strong likes and dislikes and quick to form opinions [and] unflinching in his judgments of men's acts," wrote in a letter directed to the attorney general that "if there could be *any* murder in respect of which clemency should not be exercised this is the case." The crime was large, the defendant was dangerous, and the evidence "left no shadow of room for reasonable doubt" to Thayer. Two years later, at age forty-seven, Thayer started showing signs of mental imbalance. Just before the start of the 1915 Harvard school year, "while in a state of mental aberration," he leaped into the Charles River and drowned.

Of all the communications about Bram that reached offices in Washington, a brief letter from Brooklyn sent directly to President Taft in February 1912 had perhaps the greatest effect on Bram's immediate pardon efforts. "Now what I want to ask is, if you pardon him, will you kindly see that I am protected, as I am really afraid of him. I lived with him and know his disposition and had nothing but trouble as long as he lived with me." The writer was Hattie Bram, whose husband had deserted her and their three young sons sixteen years earlier. She had not seemed so afraid when Spencer visited her in 1896 before Bram's first trial. In the 1910 federal census, she had listed herself as widowed, though she was well aware that her onetime husband was alive, in prison (Bram, more faithfully or wishfully, described himself in the census as married). In any case, Hattie's sentiments would change dramatically in the years ahead.

While Finch considered what recommendation to make to Taft, the *Boston Globe* secured the opinion of Oscar Anderson, the only former member of the *Fuller* crew the paper could locate. Anderson had made good in the ensuing years. By 1912, he was a longtime masseur and the new manager of the Butler Exercise Club in downtown Boston. "I am opposed to capital punishment," Anderson told the paper, "but I would surely oppose the granting of a pardon to Mate Bram, for in my opinion he is not a safe man to have at large."

Despite decided voices against a Bram pardon, newspapers around the country through the early months of 1912 reported the likelihood of it; it was "confidently expected" by officials of the Atlanta prison. By August, though, nothing had happened, and Bram felt compelled to write a long letter to Attorney General

Wickersham, who had met Bram earlier on a prison visit. Bram wrote as "a poor, penniless, friendless, and unfortunate creature," but "God knows I never committed the crime of which I am unfairly charged." He had been on watch and walking the deck load when "Monks called to me from the cabin and told me that the other occupants were dead. This was the first and only knowledge I had of any crimes being committed. I was unjustly accused and convicted . . . as a result of the untruthful testimony that was given against me." This was the most outspoken Bram had been about Monks in particular. Wickersham, though, did not reply.

September came around and still nothing had happened, and it appeared that nothing soon would. "I have studied over it and can myself come to no conclusion," said an unnamed official, possibly Finch, quoted in the *Boston Globe*. "The President himself would no doubt be puzzled about what to do in the matter." Bram waited.

The following March, Bram welcomed to his Atlanta cell a Bostonian who was arguably as well known as he and as unlikely a federal prisoner as one could imagine: Julian Hawthorne, sixty-six-year-old son of Nathaniel, who had died in 1864 when Julian was a Harvard freshman (he was thrown out two years later). The son was a fair journalist and writer himself, though not at his father's level, and a very bad stock promoter. A Harvard friend had convinced him to lend his prominent name to the cause of fraudulent silver mining companies; after shareholders raised an alarm, Hawthorne and his friend were convicted of mail fraud and sent to the Atlanta prison for a year.

Hawthorne was impressed by Bram, whom Hawthorne thought was likely innocent. Bram's prison record was "wholly blameless," Hawthorne wrote, and his "self-control was great . . . his manner always soft and ingratiating [and] he was politic and prudent."

Hawthorne soon made sensational charges about inhumane treatment of prisoners by warden Moyer, but if Hawthorne believed Bram a confederate, he had miscalculated. "Mr. Moyer is the most humane, just, kind, and lovable person I have ever met. In my mind there is no shadow of a doubt but that he is the best man at the head of any prison in this country." Bram said if there was any investigation based on Hawthorne's charges, Moyer "will not suffer, but will be revealed as the kind and competent official that he is."

An investigation did take place, and Moyer was found blameless, though Hawthorne turned his charges into a book, *The Subterranean Brotherhood*, that called for, among other reforms, the end to all criminal incarceration. It is possible that Bram simply calculated that denigrating Moyer would not serve Bram's efforts to get out of prison; it seems at least as likely that Bram honestly valued Moyer as a friend.

Meanwhile, Bram's incarceration had finally ended. In May 1913, a parole board, acting under a new federal law that allowed for parole of life convicts after fifteen years, recommended Bram's release. After some delays occasioned by opposing forces in Washington, he left the Atlanta prison on August 27, greeted by a crowd of supporters and press. "Brown accused me falsely," Bram told reporters. "I do not know who committed the crime. But I hope to know some day. I only know that I did not do it. The aim of my life is to find the guilty man." First, though, he was going to buy a bunch of flowers and "send them to Warden Moyer. He has been kind to me. Then I am going to get me a room and go into it by myself and have a good cry. . . . Then I'll want to pray a little. And after that I want work."

Neither Bram nor the many newspapers reporting his freedom made expressly clear just yet that this was parole, not a pardon. President Taft had avoided a difficult decision, and Bram, while free from prison, was not free from the assumption of guilt. This and the legal restrictions on a federal parolee would hamper him for years to come. As he wrote to warden Moyer the day after his release, "I do hope and pray that my innocence will be proven some day soon." Only then might he be pardoned and arguably presumed guiltless.

For the moment, a paroled Bram aroused differing opinions. "I am greatly pleased to learn that Bram is once more free," said James Cotter, who was "never satisfied that the man was guilty." He added pointedly, "There were others on that boat who could have committed the crimes." By using the plural, Cotter meant Monks as well as Brown. Dr. John Dixwell, who had supported Spencer after the killings and "never believed the statement made by Brown at the trial that he saw the murder of Captain Nash," was "sincerely glad that Bram is a free man again."

There were loud voices against Bram on the other side. "Few convicts have ever been so fortunate as this one," seethed Charles Grinnell, a Harvard-educated lawyer and legal writer and editor. "There have been showered upon him before and after his conviction," Grinnell wrote in a two-page redux of the case for the *Boston Sunday Herald*, "all the gifts that the generosity of exceptionally able counsel, the doubts of judges of the supreme court of the United States, the ingenuity of law reformers and the sympathy of philanthropists could devise and furnish." A sympathetic philanthropist Grinnell presumably had in mind was John Dixwell, whose brother-in-law Oliver Wendell Holmes Jr., along with Sherman Hoar's oldest brother, Samuel, and Ellery Sedgwick's uncle Arthur, had all preceded Grinnell as editor of the *American Law Review*. Perhaps Grinnell considered Dixwell a dilettante in legal affairs.

Grinnell, at any rate, had long espoused Bram's guilt, with a hidden reason. After the first verdict against Bram in 1897 aroused public doubts, Grinnell, who had closely observed the trial, wrote a long essay, "Why Thomas Bram Was Found Guilty," in a lawyers' magazine, seeking to silence the doubters. It was not publicly noted that Grinnell had been "engaged by the family to look after Lester's interests," which meant asserting Bram's certain guilt and nobody else's.

Once again, Oscar Anderson was available for comment, but he was more circumspect than a year earlier: "Bram is out. That is all there is to it." Saying more "would do no good and would have a tendency to injure my business." He noted again that he hadn't seen any of his former shipmates for years. "They are probably either dead or in all parts of the globe, as is liable to be the case with sailors." In fact, all of them were alive and most lived in the Boston area, but this was not a crew given to reunions.

The *Boston Post* had attempted to locate Lester Monks. "He has been much in evidence in Boston during the years which have elapsed since the murder trials, as evinced by records in the courts of business and marital troubles." Nothing of any business success was mentioned, though his absence from Boston after the divorce from his "charming" former wife was. "He is understood to be somewhere in the western part of the country," wrote the *Boston Post*, whose editors apparently had not read or figured out the recent clues in the *Atlantic*.

Meanwhile, efforts were under way to prove Bram's innocence and win him the desired exculpatory pardon. The most notable effort appeared of all places in *McClure's Magazine*, the respected illustrated monthly that published everyone from Ida Tarbell and Willa Cather to Mark Twain and Arthur Conan Doyle.

"It was the Summer of 1912, a hot, starlit night," and people were sitting on the lawn of the Allegheny Country Club, including best-selling mystery writer Mary Roberts Rinehart. The talk drifted to the sea and its mysteries, and the talkers dwindled to just Rinehart and prominent Pittsburgh lawyer Thomas Patterson. "I have often thought that there was a great story to be written around the murders on the *Herbert Fuller*," he told Rinehart, "and I also believe that in that case there was a grave miscarriage of justice."

Rinehart was intrigued and immediately set to work. She was a quick study of the trial record and other documents. The following

June, the first of five monthly installments of her novel *The After House* ran in *McClure's*. Her book was fiction, but in promotional material, she laid out the case against Bram's guilt.

First, Bram had no motive. It was alleged if anything to be piracy, but a pirate doesn't spend the opening days of a voyage alienating the crew whose support would be needed. Second, the crimes were bloody and Bram's clothes were not, nor did he make any attempt to discover if there were any incriminating stains throughout the night of the murders and into the daylight. Third, Brown's story had a major time discrepancy. He had testified that five or six minutes passed from the time he missed Bram on deck until he saw Bram return up the forward companionway. But to have accomplished all of his supposed actions in that period, Rinehart noted, Bram "could hardly have done it had he been running at the top of his speed."

Rinehart took up the story as a fiction set on a private yacht with a more attractive cast, a love angle, various deaths, and the first mate accused but a crewman eventually proven guilty, as Rinehart believed Brown was.

In her later years, Rinehart was called "the American Agatha Christie," but the reverse has never been asserted. From one of her books derives the murder mystery trope "the butler did it," and from another the inspiration for the Batman cartoon, but Rinehart's greatest service to literature was to birth two sons whom she later helped establish Farrar & Rinehart, an ancestor of a division of today's Houghton Mifflin Harcourt. Still, Rinehart was a prodigious and very popular writer, and *The After House* would be enjoyed by former president Roosevelt and then-president Wilson, both friends of hers and soon essential to Bram's fortunes.

Bram received a copy of *The After House* from publisher Roger Scaife and sent an appreciative letter of thanks in which he took the opportunity "to say to you in the presence of Almighty God that I never committed the crime for which I . . . suffered more than seventeen years behind prison bars." Bram asked Scaife to make "a private and personal appeal" to President Wilson to grant Bram a pardon. Scaife apparently felt he had done enough by publishing Rinehart's book and did not write to Wilson.

Another fan of Rinehart's book was John Dixwell. In a private note to Rinehart in April 1914, he suggested that Brown was a liar and Monks worse: "Monks, the drunken degenerate passenger, could not of course be believed because of his well known past life." These were sharp words. What, if anything, he knew about Monks's past life at the time of the *Fuller* voyage, beyond his removal from Harvard, Dr. Dixwell didn't say.

TRUE TO HIS word upon release in 1913, Bram set to praying, in public appearances at a Baptist church in Atlanta. His preaching brought tears to at least one in the congregation, a former guard at the penitentiary: "Mr. Bram, I am a better man for having heard you tonight." Bram remembered the guard for treating him less like a prisoner "but more as a brother."

True to his needs, Bram soon found work: as a shipping clerk at an Atlanta coffin factory, a position must richer in irony than the thirty dollars monthly pay, which barely covered his expenses at a modest boardinghouse. "A start," said Bram, uncomplaining, "was all I asked and I have what I asked for."

Bram rapidly improved his situation. He soon had a job at fifty dollars a month with the Southern Railway as weighmaster in their local yard, where his supervisors would attest to his excellent work and conduct: "One of the best workers I ever saw," wrote the yard master to the attorney general in 1915. Bram was ineligible, though, for promotion and better pay due to his parolee status; only a pardon would enable that.

Atlantans and their publications took up Bram's cause. "He was convicted by the evidence of a personal enemy," editorialized the *Atlantian*. "It is the testimony of every man who has come in contact with Bram, during the past nineteen years, that they have implicit faith in his innocence. . . . This innocent man should have justice done him by the Federal Government, in so far as justice can be done a man for such a wrong, by the granting of an unconditional pardon."

In October 1915, Bram wrote a long letter to President Wilson, petitioning for a pardon. "The evidence which fastened upon me the conviction of a crime, which God in Heaven knows I never committed, and could never have committed, was absolutely circumstantial, and was given by men who held an enmity against me, their Superior Officer, and all of whom swore falsely against me that the crime might not be laid at the door of any one of them." For "all these long dreary years," Bram had daily "prayed that the perpetrator of the crime might become concience [*sic*] stricken and make his confession, thereby proving me innocent before man, as I know I am before God."

Wilson apparently did not respond directly, but communications between Bram supporters, including his parole officer, and officials in Washington continued for several months until pardon attorney Finch seemed to put a stop to all efforts in early February 1916. Bram had been on parole for two and a half years; for a pardon in a capital case, Finch reminded various correspondents, "five years' probation is required." He was impressed with Bram's record in prison and since, but, Finch informed the head of the federal parole board, "murder is one of the greatest crimes" and a pardon application was "premature now."

Bram, meanwhile, moved forward. If the lack of a pardon restricted his advancement as an employee, it didn't impede him immediately as an owner. In late 1915, "I left the Railroad and went into the lunch business." That is, a small soda fountain and lunch counter, at the corner of Marietta and Broad Streets in the heart of Atlanta. It was work he had some experience in from his years with Dennett's and in prison. Soon he opened a second place a few blocks away on Decatur Street.

Despite the five-year parole period before a pardon could be considered, Bram supporters persisted, and detractors resisted. In March 1916, Attorney General Thomas Watt Gregory, reacting to various entreaties from influential Bram supporters, asked Finch to gather materials and report. "I see no special hurry about it and you will therefore take it up when more pressing matters permit." Finch took Gregory at his word; four months later, Gregory repeated his request.

In November 1916, Assistant Attorney General Charles Warren reported to Gregory that no consideration at all should be given Bram. "I was present at the trial, and the evidence satisfied me that Bram was an extremely dangerous man. I believe that he has some mental or degenerate quality which will undoubtedly lead him to commit another murder."

Warren, a Boston-born graduate of Harvard College (1889) and Harvard Law (1892), knew a degenerate menace when he perceived one. In 1894, he had cofounded with two Harvard classmates the Immigration Restriction League that advocated with great influence against "undesirable" non-Anglo-Saxon Europeans as racially inferior. Flush with nativist and eugenicist fervor, league membership was primarily Boston Brahmins and graduates of Harvard, including its longest-serving president, Eliot, and other leading academics, such as Stanford founding president David Starr Jordan. For good measure, Warren opposed voting rights for women and during the Great War saw spies everywhere, especially in the melting pot of New York City.

It was an outrage to Warren that Bram was free even on parole. "If I had been in the Department at the time when the parole was granted, I should have opposed parole with the greatest earnestness, and I believe that his present release on parole is a distinct menace to society." Warren later wrote several well-regarded texts on the Constitution and the Supreme Court; his marriage of fifty years produced no offspring to perpetuate or reject his extreme social beliefs.

Attorney General Gregory also heard from the other side. "Many of my personal friends who know Mr. Bram advise me," wrote Senator Thomas Hardwick in January 1917, "that he is a most excellent gentleman and thoroughly worthy of a pardon." Hardwick, a Georgia Democrat, interestingly enough was a sponsor of the Immigration Act of 1918, a product of Warren's nativist agenda, but he managed to see Bram's plight clearly.

FOR THE TIME being, the anti-Bram forces won the day. In February 1917, Attorney General Gregory recommended a pardon denial; three months later, President Wilson followed Gregory's recommendation. In the spring of 1917, Wilson was involved with more pressing matters.

Bram could only bide his time, making money in the Atlanta food business and hoping that his cause for exoneration would mature. At the same time, Lester Monks set about trying to make something of his new life. Meanwhile, the thing that tied their lives together disappeared.

9

REDEMPTION

... the closing chapter of a wonderful case.
—Thomas Bram, *Boston Globe*, June 19, 1919

G ustav Siess lined up his shot. A native son of Hamburg, Kapitänleutnant Siess was the new commander of U-33. Siess,
thirty-three himself, was a prolific sinker of enemy ships—military,
commercial, or otherwise. Commanding a different U-boat a few
months earlier, Siess set the mine that sank the *Britannic*, younger
sister of the also sinkable *Titanic*. U-33 under Siess and a prior
commander had sent to the bottom scores of vessels large and
small, including a Russian hospital ship, protected by the Hague
Convention but torpedoed nonetheless, killing dozens of Red
Cross workers and crew.

Siess's target this day was the *Margaret B. Rouss*, a three-masted
schooner bound from St. Andrews Bay on the Florida panhandle to Genoa, Italy, with a full load of pitch-pine lumber. It was
April 27, 1917. Siess had no idea that this next kill, his second of the
day, was no ordinary old sailing ship, a relatively slow-moving, vul-
nerable elder amid the new century's agile machines of war. Siess
was ending the life of a ship infamous for savagery, and he visited

on it fitting indignities. Of fifty-six ships sunk by Siess during World War I, the *Margaret B. Rouss* was his only American kill.

The *Rouss*, under Captain Frederick L. Foote, had sailed from St. Andrews on February 4. At Key West two weeks later, Foote received a reply to his earlier telegram to Secretary of State Robert Lansing, requesting advice on the safety in war waters of ships flying the flag of the United States, still a neutral country. Lansing wired back that the rights of American vessels had not changed and that "a neutral vessel may, if its owner believes it liable to unlawful attack, take any necessary measure to prevent or resist such attacks." How an unarmed sailing ship was supposed to resist U-boat or other attacks Lansing had nothing to say. Two months into the voyage, and apparently unknown to Captain Foote and his crew of seven as they crossed the Atlantic and put in at Gibraltar, the United States declared war on Germany, on April 6.

A week later, Friday, the thirteenth—a very bad day to put to sea—the *Margaret B. Rouss* started into the Mediterranean on the last leg of the journey. Just after 6:00 p.m. two Fridays later, forty-five sea miles south of Monaco and just fifty miles short of completing the fifty-nine-hundred-mile voyage from Florida, the *Rouss*'s starboard side planking amidships was ripped open by what Foote understood could only have been a U-boat torpedo. Seawater poured in; the old ship foundered. With darkness approaching, captain and crew successfully launched their lifeboat, bringing aboard what supplies and navigational tools they could.

The attack by a modern warship—one invisible beneath the surface to its target—on a defenseless merchant sailing ship carrying only lumber was bad enough, but the survivors and their vessel were then subject to humiliation all too traditional on the sea. Its cargo being buoyant lumber, the *Rouss* did not sink, at least quickly enough for Kapitänleutnant Siess. He surfaced his sub and with five crewmen launched and rowed a boat over to the resistant ship. Ordering Captain Foote to stand by in their lifeboat, the Germans boarded the *Rouss* and in the course of two hours of fading light rummaged the cabins and storerooms for all the loot of any value they could fit in their boat. Still not content, Siess rowed over to Foote and, "like pirates of the olden days," relieved the Americans of every loose article they had: money, tobacco, pipes, food, and, for good measure, the ship's charts and compass and Foote's sextant, chronometer, and fountain pen. Then, as the Americans watched, Siess rowed back to the *Rouss* and had his men place bombs in her hold and finally blow apart and sink her, ending for good the ship's twenty-seven years afloat. Captain Foote and his crew were allowed to row away on a fortunately calm night sea to Monaco, where the prince and, as it happened, visiting American newspaper tycoon James Gordon Bennett took good care of them and booked them safer passage back to the United States.

A month later, Foote was home in Queens, New York, telling his story to reporters and vowing to get back to Europe in an armed ship and somehow find and take vengeance on Gustav Siess. More reasonably, Foote announced his intention to persuade the authorities of his South Ozone Park neighborhood to change the name of his street: Kaiser Avenue. Foote never got to Siess, who served in Germany's next war and died peacefully in 1970, but he did get his second wish: by 1919, Kaiser Avenue became 142nd Place, as it remains today.

The violent end of the *Margaret B. Rouss* was fitting. Five years earlier, her new owners had refitted her as a schooner from her original rig as a barkentine and abandoned her original name, *Herbert Fuller*.

The *Fuller* had sailed many miles since 1896, not without incident. A day short of two years after the murders, Manuel Murillo, a Portuguese seaman, fell from the mizzenmast in a gale off the US east coast and was lost in the heavy sea. "Ill Luck Follows the Fuller," observed the *Brooklyn Daily Eagle*. During her next voyage came fears that the ship, weeks late to Brazil with no word after seventy-four days from New York, had been lost; a hurricane had recently crossed her intended path. The ship with all hands accounted for materialized soon after. Sailing for New York from the Florida panhandle in February 1900 with a load of lumber, the *Fuller* arrived off Sandy Hook in a winter storm, was blown out to sea sixty miles, and, sails and rigging frozen and bows heavy with accumulating ice, went perilously "down by the head" before making her way into the harbor. The crew was frostbitten, but no fingers were lost. The following winter, the ship was at an East River pier in New York when a laborer fell into the hold, sustaining "serious injuries." To say the *Herbert Fuller* had more than its share of mishaps would be unfair; to say that reporters and the public seemed to be alert to any news about the infamous ship would not. Some news was less than it seemed. On June 24, 1897, while Bram's Supreme Court appeal was pending, the *New York Times* saw fit to print on page 1 that the steward who had been aboard for the murders had drowned in Halifax: "He has been drinking heavily of late," the paper observed. The *Times* apparently had forgotten that the *Fuller's* famous steward was Jonathan Spencer, who was still safely ashore in New York; the dead man was John Taylor, who had joined the ship in 1897.

Regardless of the ship's occasional troubles, the *Fuller* sailed and made money for her owners until 1910, when a dockside fire caused substantial damage to the rigging and other gear. Repair costs were estimated at $7,000. Two weeks after the fire, Herbert Fuller didn't want "to put any more money into the vessel" that bore his name. Preferences varied among the many owners, but most thought the time had come to sell. "She has been a bad egg from the word go," decided one owner who favored a sale. Among the Rays, Laura's mother and her two younger brothers, Irv and George, all preferred a sale to costly repairs and likely continued unprofitability. Various Nashes agreed.

By 1912, the ship had been sold for $32,000, what must have seemed like a windfall to the former owners. The new owner put the ship back to sea, under his daughter's name, Margaret Baltzell Rouss, "one of the most attractive girls of society . . . and one of the best horsewomen of her day." She married a rich coal merchant in 1916 and started having children; there is no record if she knew that her ship went down the following year.

The sinking of the former *Herbert Fuller* was widely reported; among many newspaper accounts of the ship's earlier notoriety, the *Boston Herald* in particular noted "Negro mate" Bram and "Harvard student" Monks. Presumably, each was aware of this epilogue to one aspect of their common history.

———◆◆◆———

LESTER MONKS, NEWLY remarried in June 1917 and set up in a Manhattan townhouse, was uncertain of his next step. For a while, as recalled by his young cousin Gardner, then attending the Union Theological Seminary in New York, Lester was promoting "Dory Stores," a prospective chain of boat-themed retail shops selling fish and produce. It appears the idea went out with the first tide.

Soon enough, old Harvard and Boston shipping connections paid off. By late 1917, Monks was on the board of the Boston-based Shawmut Steamship Company, which operated cargo ships in partnership with the US Navy. Harvard men dominated the company that had been established in 1914.

Lester, as a company vice president and with wife Caroline, attended the late September 1917 launch of a Shawmut freighter, the four-hundred-foot *Sudbury*, at a yard on the Delaware River. A few months later, he was advertising his services in maritime securities out of a downtown Manhattan office—"Information Cheerfully Furnished"—while retaining a position on the Shawmut board; in July 1919, Mrs. Monks christened another Shawmut freighter.

Later that year, Monks took a big step up, becoming the president of W. A. Harriman & Co., a newly formed shipping concern founded and funded by the much younger Averill Harriman, the Yale-educated future icon of American business, politics, and diplomacy. Harriman was chairman of the board; the roster of executives included an Adams, a Rockefeller, and George Peabody Gardner, Lester's cousin by marriage.

Monks found himself in this rarified company, with a large salary but lesser decision-making authority. The Harriman company took over the widespread freight and passenger services of the Germany-based Hamburg-American Line, the largest shipping company in the world before its routes were suspended at the start of war in 1914. At the same time, Harriman's company acquired a controlling interest in the American Ship and Commerce Corporation, which had been operating the German company's freight route between Hamburg and New York. Monks was named a director of American Ship, while Harriman himself became president (displacing Panama Canal chief engineer and decorated federal wartime shipping administrator George Goethals).

The arrangements between these and related companies and the socially and politically connected men who ran them was (and remains) murky to those on the outside. By mid-1920, the Harriman-controlled group consisted of a half-dozen interrelated maritime companies, including builders, shippers, and insurers. A profile of Monks in an insurance industry publication noted that the Harriman group had quickly become "one of the largest ever put through in American history and will mean much to the future development and stability of the American merchant marine." Young Harriman's brilliant career was launching, and the older Monks's career rode with it.

For a bit.

AT THE TIME of the destruction of the former *Herbert Fuller*, Thomas Bram was focused on his current legal status, bitterly disappointed by President Wilson's 1917 pardon denial but hardly daunted. By late 1917, he was doing $2,000 a month in business at his lunch counters, clearing $400, banking at two major Atlanta banks, and giving to various charities. It had been up to him "to prove my worthiness" when he was released on parole, he wrote to pardon attorney Finch, "and I do hope that I have done this." He was also, he informed Finch, in the process of purchasing a house, and he was getting married, to "a pure and lofty-minded woman," a forty-year-old "old maid" named Emma Louise Smith. At some point during his imprisonment, his first wife had finally secured a divorce.

In this first in a series of letters to Finch over the next year and a half, the parolee was clearly attempting to win the pardon attorney's favor. "Should I transgress the rules of propriety in communicating with you without first obtaining permission from you to do so," Bram opened his letter, "when you learn the cause of my action, I am sure that your kind heart will forgive me for so doing."

Bram reiterated what he had said for many years: "I was unjustly accused of the crime of murder . . . a crime I know nothing of and one which I could not have committed." Now he had additional cause for a pardon: "In justice to the good woman whom I hope to marry shortly, I would like to have the disability removed from me, and I once more be declared a free man." Bram asked Finch to ask the attorney general to reconsider his case. For good measure, he added, "Please grant me the privilege of sending you a piece of wedding cake shortly."

Bram's marriage didn't happen until the following March, so Finch didn't have to respond to the cake offer. More immediately, Bram informed Finch in mid-1918 that he had added a third and substantially larger restaurant and was now clearing more than $800 a month.

Bram's big break came with the appointment of a new attorney general in March 1919. The day after Emma Smith became Bram's second wife, A. Mitchell Palmer, namesake of the unfortunate

Palmer Raids later that year, asked Finch for a report on Bram and a week later recommended to Wilson a pardon.

"It should not be lost sight of," Palmer reported to Wilson, that Bram "was convicted solely on circumstantial evidence." Finch had conceded to Palmer that though he considered Bram "probably guilty," he had "never been able to reach a satisfactory conclusion." For his part, Palmer believed "there must always be some element of doubt as to whether or not Bram was really guilty of the crime." That, together with Bram's "record for good conduct since release on parole, and the esteem in which he is held by all who know him," convinced Palmer that Bram was owed a pardon and restoration of his full civil rights. The president, otherwise deeply engaged in France with the Versailles Treaty and perhaps distracted, followed the recommendation and granted Bram's pardon on April 22, 1919.

In his memorandum to Wilson, Attorney General Palmer had referred to Bram as "a colored man." This was perhaps the first time in nearly a quarter century since the *Fuller* murders that Bram had been formally identified in a way that he never acknowledged.

Bram did not make an issue of Palmer's racial characterization. Instead, he focused on Wilson's act. As far as Thomas Bram was concerned, this was a "full and unconditional pardon," and that was all that mattered. In a letter to his trial lawyers, declaring himself "your innocent client," he rejoiced at "the closing chapter of a wonderful case."

Not everyone considered Bram's pardon wonderful. Assistant Attorney General Claude Porter, a dedicated hunter of spies and communists, and nine-time loser for Iowa governor and US senator, lamented that "lapse of time always paves the way for doubt as to the guilt of a man." As far as Porter was concerned, two federal judges and juries could not have found an innocent man guilty. Still, in his outraged memorandum to the attorney general, Porter couldn't help but get tripped up: at the second trial, he typed,

"Because one juror held out he was given a life sentence." Apparently realizing he might be misunderstood, Porter crossed out "he" and handwrote "the defendant." Porter let stand his error that in fact the vote before the jury's decision to give a life sentence was not eleven to one but nine to three, as it had been before the first jury's decision to find Bram guilty and give him death.

Many people, especially in Atlanta and Boston, were gratified that Bram had finally been fully cleared; others shook their heads. But as the *Boston Globe* reminded everyone, Bram's "pardon again brings up the question: who was the murderer of Capt Nash, his wife, and Mate Bromberg [*sic*] if Bram wasn't?"

10

JOYS AND SORROWS

... one of those unfathomable mysteries destined to
discussion ... until the death of the last person holding
it in memory.
—*Boston Globe*, January 28, 1929

For all the hope of a midlife rebirth, Lester Monks could not
escape his past. It pursued him. At some point during the time
he was forging a new life in shipping, he traveled to Washington
on related business. There he happened to attend an informal afternoon party at the home of Leita and Edward White. White
had been the chief justice of the US Supreme Court since 1910,
when he was elevated from the associate justice seat he had held
since 1894; in 1897, White had written the opinion giving Thomas
Bram a new trial.

Lester was welcomed at the door by Mrs. White. Her husband, a large man, was nearby, in deep conversation with another
guest. Mrs. White reached up to tap the chief justice's shoulder.
"Edward, you will want to shake hands with our old friend, Lester Monks." The chief justice caught only the last words. "Lester
Monks!" he said. "Yes, I always believed he did it." "Incidents like

this," recalled his friend Ellery Sedgwick, "perturbing to ordinary folk, slipped from Lester like water from a duck's back."

Another suggestion of Monks's guilt arose some years later. Even after his pardon, Bram wrote with some regularity to his former lawyers. On July 30, 1921, a letter to French relayed Bram's usual "undying gratitude" to French and Cotter, "as fresh and lasting as the day you both first met me." He also had some incredible news: one of his prison attorneys, prominent Atlantan William Schley Howard, had been told by pardon attorney Finch that the Justice Department "has a dying confession letter from Monks who died in California, exonerating me fully." Bram said that Howard was attempting to get a copy of the confession.

Neither French nor Cotter apparently responded to this astounding news. Nor did a copy of the dying confession letter ever reach Bram or anyone else. There appears to be no such letter in any government archive; nor does one evidently reside in Howard's surviving papers, such as they are held by a granddaughter in unsorted boxes.

The likely reason that a dying Monks 1921 confession from California has not turned up is that Monks did not die in 1921. Nor was he in California in 1921, or apparently ever. In fact, he was still in New York City, doing shipping business out of his office on Wall Street and living with his second wife at 18 West Ninth Street. They had lived there since their marriage in June 1917 and would remain there until late 1922, when she sold the house and they moved to Boston.

A Monks confession seems an unlikely thing for either Bram or reputable and proper Howard to have made up in 1921, two years after Bram had been pardoned. He was leading a normal life, his name was effectively cleared, and he was free in his remaining years to make what he could of them. As for Monks, his false 1921 death proved an omen.

The Roaring Twenties might have been Lester Monks's big decade. Recently married to a wealthy woman, with a young daughter by her, a fashionable address, and a close association with a rising star of American commerce, Lester Monks was no longer the former passenger on a murder ship (and a former railroad construction laborer) but a mature businessman whose opinions mattered. In 1920, at age thirty, William Averill Harriman was "the new shipping king of America," and Lester Monks, reborn at forty-four, was by his side. Harriman, wrote the *Boston Post* in a company profile, had "a larger interest in American shipping than any other man in America" and his business partner Monks likened their many companies to a "huge transatlantic shipping 'pie.'"

That was in July; in October, Monks was out. He had resigned from Harriman & Co., reportedly "to devote all his time strictly to American ships and shipping." The *Times* reported that the break was "amicable, that he will act in an advisory capacity." In fact, his old business relations continued and merged. The following January, his first business partner, George Warren, formed the Warren Export Coal Company, with Warren as president, Harriman as chairman, and, incredibly after their break thirteen years earlier, Monks as a vice president.

Against all odds, Monks was suddenly astride two great shipping interests. A few weeks later, he was on board the White Star liner *Adriatic* headed to eight European countries for two months of coal business. A year later, Monks and Warren oversaw the purchase of a fleet of coal-carrying steamships, to be operated out of Boston by a Harriman-affiliated company. Later in 1922, Caroline sold the Manhattan townhouse, and she, Lester, their young daughter, and Lester's son, David, from his first marriage, took up residence on Boston's Beacon Hill.

WHAT MIGHT HAVE been a business rebirth in his home territory soon enough went bad. "For quite a while, he stayed off the bottle," observed his cousin, but "the deadly chain reaction started up again: from business turn-down to drinking to bad decisions to worse business to total blotto. The pattern of fifteen years before was repeating itself."

While Monks remained with Warren Export in some capacity, another venture proved to be his undoing. For several years, he had been involved with the Pacific Development Company, which had been formed in 1917 to do importing, exporting, and general industrial development in the Orient (as the region was then called). "I looked over the world during the war to see where investment could be made farthest away from Germany and the European debacle," he told financial journalist Clarence Barron in March 1924. "Looking right through the world, I selected China as farthest away from Europe and offering greatest opportunity for development and put my money into the Pacific Development Company. Now China is the worst spot in the world and going like Russia."

Chief among the company's dealings was a loan of $5.5 million to the increasingly unstable government of the faltering Chinese republic. By early 1922, the Chinese had failed to make any repayments; by midyear an arrangement to start paying just interest without principal fell apart. By January 1925, Pacific Development was in receivership, with $12 million in liabilities.

As with most of his business dealings, Monks's role in Pacific Development is opaque, but its failure was his last substantial business involvement. It seems he remained with Warren Export as a courtesy. He kept offices in the Monks Building but rarely was there. "When he left the house, [his wife] would never know when or in what condition he would reappear. Sometimes it would be a week or more before he would be brought home largely unconscious, by the police or someone else." Their daughter "as a measure of protection" was sent to live with friends on Cape Cod. There was also the time at a relative's vacation home that, according to a cousin, he climbed into bed with a sleeping niece; she was a child and he nearly fifty and increasingly erratic in behavior.

In March 1926, Lester's father died, at seventy-five, at the family home in Brookline. Obituaries noted his business achievements and social connections. Lester was mentioned briefly along with the other relatives. There was nothing about the *Herbert Fuller* or Frank Monks's efforts to keep his son out of legal trouble after the murders.

Already drinking heavily and doing little business before his father's death, Lester was staggered in February 1927 by a widely syndicated two-page spread in the *New York Daily News*. "When Justice Triumphed," ran the headline over a recent large photo of a well-dressed Thomas Bram and a long retelling of the *Herbert Fuller* story. The triumph of justice, according to the feature article, was Bram's parole, pardon, and current business success in Atlanta. The writer did not point fingers at Monks or anyone else but clearly presented Bram as innocent and vindicated, leaving informed readers no choice but Brown or Monks.

Six months later, during the evening of September 9, 1927, Lester was out drinking. Sometime before midnight, he collapsed in the lane in front of his home on Beacon Hill. He was found and brought inside. Dr. Worcester was called. He and Caroline stood vigil. It had been "her constant hope and wish that he should die at home in his own bed," and he did, during the early morning.

There was no public notice, not even a paid obituary. The body was cremated and the remains interred in the family mausoleum at Forest Hills Cemetery, the garden necropolis on the fringe of Boston where Cabots and Lowells talk to God forever. Lester Monks, though, who had recently been among—or at least publicly associated with—the foremost leaders of American business, was to disappear unacknowledged.

Somehow, the *Boston Globe* got wind of the news: "L. H. Monks' Death Recalls Sea Crime" was the headline on page 28 on September 13, the day after the otherwise unreported and very private funeral service. The *Globe* story recalled "one of the most celebrated criminal cases in the history of America." It was filled with errors, about the killings and especially Monks: the paper said he came from "a family of shipowners," got his Harvard degree in 1898, and in 1911 "gave up much of his coal interests and went to British Columbia, working on railway construction until 1915," as if this had been business and not banishment plus manual labor. The death was said to have been heart failure at his home; alcohol was not mentioned.

Following the trend by then in other latter-day accounts of the *Herbert Fuller* murders, guilt was not assigned to anyone, including Bram: "Never obtrusive [*sic*], he gradually came to be a highly respected business man." As to Monks's character, the *Globe* took no position. It did mention that the funeral service was officiated by the Reverend Gardner Monks, who might have said graveside something similar to the final judgment in his memoirs on Lester: "His was a life filled to overflowing with both success and failure, with tragedy and achievement, with joys and sorrows caused and borne."

⚬

WHAT NO RELATIVE, friend, or former shipmate would say is that Lester Monks's life was irrevocably shaped thirty years earlier aboard the *Herbert Fuller*. The murders—that family lawyer Bartlett and Chief Justice White knew were his and that he lied about at trial—worked corrosively on Lester, ultimately isolating him, unable to reveal his secret. The drinking gave him comfort and, eventually, mercy.

Conflicts and uncertainty about Lester survive. The death certificate I requested and received from the Boston city registrar, number 537216, says that Lester H. Monks died on September 9, 1927, at age fifty-one of cardiovascular disorder. It also says that he was female. I contacted the registrar and pointed out the greater and lesser errors. A week later, I received number 540950, largely correct: death on September 10, age fifty-one years, four months, thirteen days, the cause cardiovascular disorder "associated with use of alcohol," his sex male. I didn't ask either how it was possible to have so many errors or omissions the first time around and what was the source for the corrective information about cause.

———— ⬥ ————

LESTER'S SON, DAVID, was sent by his stepfather to grammar and boarding schools. In 1923, Lester Monks wrote in his Harvard Class of 1898 report, "I trust and hope my son David Park Monks will go to Cambridge this coming fall." Keeping his distance, David went to Princeton and graduated in 1925. He then worked as a stock and bond broker and, long after his father's death, in 1935 married Marion Neel, two years his elder, from a fashionable Philadelphia suburb. Reverend Monks officiated at the wedding, as he had eight years earlier at the funeral of David's father. The newlyweds honeymooned on Bermuda and initially lived in the old family home in Brookline with his widowed stepmother and her and Lester's then young daughter, Caroline. Within a few years, David and Marion had relocated; eventually, they divorced.

"Fortunately there were no children," observed Reverend Monks after David's early death in 1958. "Drinking habits recurred, and, like his father, he died a hopeless alcoholic." Officially, it was hepatic cirrhosis, the body was cremated, and David became the last Monks inhumed in the family mausoleum at Forest Hills. David Monks was also the last carrier of the Monks name in Lester's stunted branch of the family tree.

Lester's widow, Caroline, lived quietly for many years and died at sixty-three in 1953; she is buried beside her husband. Their daughter, Caroline, after boarding schools, went to Vassar and in 1946, following a courtship interrupted by war, married very happily a Princeton and Harvard graduate who became a popular Brown math professor for forty years. Of her in his fortieth undergraduate reunion book, he quoted Proverbs: "A good wife is to be valued above rubies." She died in 1991, he in 2011; their only child, born decades after the death of his grandfather, knows him only as a bad growth in the family tree.

Lester's grandson and only direct survivor, now in his sixties, is an intelligent, well-spoken, gentle soul, a cofounder of a radical queer intentional community and retreat center in rural Northern California. There will be no next generation. Lester Monks's line will end. In legacy as in life, he will remain not fully knowable: an exclamation point twisted by time and circumstance into a question mark.

———◈———

"I AM INNOCENT," Thomas Bram had told reporters the day he was convicted in 1897. "When I die it will be as God intended. Naturally, I know that I will never be hanged." Just four months after the death of Lester Monks in September 1927, it seemed that God was making his intentions clear. "Slayer of Three Lost With Ship" ran the headline in the *New York Sun*, above the Associated Press story carried by papers across the country. In the excitement, the fact of Bram's exonerating pardon was temporarily forgotten.

It seemed that Bram had gone down in a Cape Hatteras gale with the *Alvena*, a four-masted schooner he had recently acquired and captained. An aging but well-built ship launched in California in 1901, the *Alvena* at 186 feet was slightly larger than the *Herbert Fuller* and with her windjammer rig a good bit quicker. Running lumber between Jacksonville, Florida—to where Bram had moved a year earlier with his new wife, Emma, to take up the sea again—and Portland, Maine, in January 1928, the ship had sent a distress signal on the eighth. Coast Guard cutters went out to search but found nothing.

Opinions varied about Bram's apparent fate. Said some: his old crime had been expiated, that retribution had finally come, that the toll of the sea had been paid. The *Atlanta Constitution* generously recalled the popular former local prisoner jailed "for a crime said to have been committed by another man." The *New York Sun* editorialized that the "loss of Mate Bram off Hatteras is the second tragic postscript to be written to this story." The other was the sinking of what had been the *Herbert Fuller* in 1917. The *Sun*, as with all of the country's papers, didn't mention and probably was unaware of Lester Monks's recent death, arguably more tragic than the bloodless scuttling of an old ship.

Since the *Alvena* distress call, "there has been silence, a silence that the ancient mariners along the waterfront feel convinced will continue." Ancient mariners and others were wrong. On the thirteenth, Bram sailed into Portland, his ship and her lumber cargo intact. All he had done, Bram told reporters, was ask a passing steamer to send a radio message "as a precautionary measure" that the *Alvena*'s pumps were out of commission. As it happened, the storm moved on, the ship stayed dry, and Bram arrived in port on schedule and surprised at the fears for his safety.

As with his presumed death, Bram's astonishing survival was reported around the country. Most papers recounted his history; one, the Bram-friendly *Atlanta Constitution*, mistakenly reported that the Wilson pardon nine years earlier had come "after a sailor in Los Angeles, on his death bed, confessed to the murder." The confession myth, born in Atlanta earlier in the decade, lingered like a faulty tale of mythic treasure.

Bram spoke little about the *Alvena* incident; he was more interested in getting on with his now profitable life in coastal shipping. "The land holds little to his liking," the *Boston Globe* reported a year later. "His remaining days will be spent on the sea." Despite the weather risks, it was an easy life for an old captain.

The *Alvena* mostly ran the Jacksonville–Portland route, on a long-term charter by a Portland lumber company; three months after his near disaster, Bram broke a twenty-year record by making a run to Maine in just eight and a half days. "Today he is a free man," the *Globe* observed, "respected by his brokers and agents and by seamen who know of his ability." He was also "spoken well of" by his crew, according to the *Globe* reporter who visited the ship in Portland in 1929. "They were dining on roast chicken in the galley, a delicacy not served on every lumber boat." As for Captain Bram, he said only, "I am innocent and always have been, and have tried to live an honest life."

As Bram's years of freedom lengthened, he fell out of touch with his lawyers. In August 1933, James Cotter died peacefully at age eighty-six in his Boston home, leaving three unmarried daughters; his wife and two other unmarried daughters had died before him. He had a varied and successful law career in and around the city, as well as numerous charitable and public affiliations, but the many obituaries focused almost entirely on the Bram case. The *New York Times* noted that Cotter was "long regarded as one of the ranking counselors of New England," and his defense of Bram was "a masterpiece." "Sea Mystery Recalled by Cotter Death" was the *Hartford Courant* headline over the Associated Press wire story, an indication that thirty-five years later the case remained more of a mystery than a tragedy. After the eventual deaths of his unmarried daughters, there were no Cotter survivors.

At the time of Cotter's death, Bram's other lawyer was having remarkable troubles. In September 1930, three years after his wife, Elisabeth, died, Asa French had married Isabel (or Isabelle) May Donaldson, the daughter of a Boston real estate developer. French was seventy, Donaldson forty-nine. They had known each other for many years. In fact, they had a son, Palmer Donaldson French, born in 1916 while Asa was still married to Elisabeth, and raised quietly by his mother.

According to Palmer French, his mother had met French when she consulted him about divorcing her first husband, a flamboyant real estate broker who ultimately died bankrupt in 1927. Asa and Isabel's 1930 wedding took place in Albany, secretly they had hoped, to protect their teenage "love child." The newspapers found out, though; so did French's grown children, not from their father but from reporters. The *Boston Globe* politely referred to the romance as "a long courtship" and did not mention their teenage son who was present for the nuptials.

Their secret romance had been long, but the honeymoon was brief. Within a month, Isabel later alleged, French had been sufficiently cruel and abusive "to warrant her living apart from him." Three Septembers later, she was seeking a divorce and money. French, in turn, claimed a prenuptial agreement enjoined any claim; at the same time, French's older children had him declared incompetent based on "his advanced age"—merely seventy-three—and a guardian was appointed.

By November 1933, French was in a sanatorium, and Isabel's claim had been dismissed in probate court. He died two years later, after his "brilliant legal career" was ended, discreetly, by "a long illness." There was no recounting of his secret life. Isabel died without notice in 1941. Palmer French attended art schools and Harvard, married three times and had numerous children, and gravitated to the 1960s art scene in San Francisco, where he died in 1990.

The news of French's disability in late 1933 reached Richard Hale, cofounder of the then and now prominent Boston law firm bearing his name. As leading members of the local legal community, Hale and French knew each other well. French's sudden infirmity, not to mention his domestic travails, was a topic of discussion among fellow lawyers, especially those who had a connection to French's most famous case, the Bram trials. In December, Hale wrote a brief letter to Eldon James, then midway through two decades in charge of the Harvard Law School library. The library was soon to acquire French's copy of the Bram trial transcripts, the only extant volumes.

Hale thought James should know something about Lester Monks: "On his death-bed he said to Professor Alfred Worcester of the [Harvard] Hygiene Department that his testimony at the murder trial was a story made up by himself."

What specifically Monks had made up Hale didn't say. The suggestion is everything: a made-up story. Back in 1921, when Monks was still quite alive, Bram had written of a deathbed confession by Monks in California. Now, twelve years later, came the assertion that Monks had indeed made a confession on his actual deathbed in 1927. In 1921, Bram had cited his Atlanta lawyer as the source; the supposed document never materialized. Now, the eminently reputable Richard Hale cited Monks's own relative, the also reputable Worcester: "Worcester told me yesterday and I don't think he would object to having this postscript pasted in to some report of the trial." Hale's letter is indeed pasted into the inside cover of the first volume of the transcript of the first trial, in the Harvard Law School library.

As it turned out, Worcester did object, more than five years later. "I was intimate with the Monks family," Worcester informed Harvard librarian James in March 1939 by letter, also pasted into the trial volume, "and at intervals after the trials Lester Monks was a patient of mine." As we know, Worcester was intimate with the Monks family via marriage: his wife's sister was married to Lester's uncle Robert. This is how Worcester came to be Lester's doctor after the trials.

In his letter to James, Worcester wrote that Lester "was supposed to be in perfect health, but he was found dead in his bed at his home on West Cedar St. Boston, on Sept. 10, 1927." This is not true. Lester was found dying in the alley outside his home, and "perfect health" does not include chronic alcoholism. Worcester knew that Lester was an alcoholic and that his last years were of such concern to his family that his daughter was sent away.

Worcester's letter continues: "Any death-bed statement, to me or any one else, was therefore quite innocent in fact. He never at any time told me that the testimony he gave at the trials of Bram was a story made up by himself, and I am sure I never told anyone that he had told me anything of the sort." That he would have lied about Lester's "perfect health" suggests that Worcester would also lie about Hale's assertion. Arguably, Worcester's lies were to protect the family's reputation, but truth is thicker than blood.

BRAM SAILED THE *Alvena* on the Florida–Maine run well into the 1930s. In December 1934, they had a close call, towed to safety by a Coast Guard cutter after a gale shredded the schooner's sails off the tip of Cape Cod. The following winter, approaching Portland in another gale, the *Alvena* struck the government light ship marking the harbor approach; Bram's ship sustained considerable damage. That year Bram turned seventy-two.

Soon enough, Bram confounded the *Globe*'s prediction that he would remain at sea until his death. In June 1939, he sold the *Alvena*, which was to be converted into a "dine and dance" ship by the new owner. Later the ship was sold to the Canadian Navy, which used it as a floating target before blowing it up on a beach. This was a similar but arguably kinder end than the *Herbert Fuller* experienced.

Selling off his ship was just one piece of a dramatic change for Bram. He also, in very quick fashion, divorced Emma in 1940, left Jacksonville, moved back to Brooklyn, and, at age seventy-six, married for a third time. His new wife was seventy-four. She was also his first wife.

Somehow, Hattie Bram's concerns for her safety communicated to President Taft back in 1912 had lessened dramatically nearly three decades later. And her wistful longing for Bram in 1896, just after the murders, had finally been satisfied: he had come back, she had forgiven him, and they took up life together again. On January 6, 1941, they married, fifty-five years after their first coupling. Within weeks, they were in Miami, in a house shared with their eldest son, William, an installer for Western Electric, and his wife, Teresa.

On the last day of March 1947, the *Miami News* briefly noted the death the previous morning of an eighty-three-year-old "retired real estate broker" at his home on Southwest Nineteenth Street, leaving his wife and their three adult sons: "He had lived in Miami six years, coming from Brooklyn, N.Y." It could have been a notice on the passing of a typical New York retiree, finishing his days in the relative warmth of Florida, the emerging boomland. The item said nothing about Thomas Bram's busy life outside of real estate. His death certificate says he was born in British Guiana, that his parents' names and birthplaces were "unobtainable," and that he was white. Hattie, who had learned otherwise about his race fifty-one years earlier, apparently was complicit in this final posturing and the associated incorrect and withheld information.

Whatever great secrets Bram held he took with him; if he told anything to his wife or any of their three sons, they didn't tell. All of them are long gone. Harriet died in 1952 and is buried in Minneapolis, where her youngest son, Herbert, lived. He died there in 1966, predeceased by his wife; there were no children. William died in Florida in 1962, his wife a year later. Walter died in Minnesota in 1973, his wife two years earlier. No survivors bear the Bram name.

When he was released from prison on parole in 1913, Thomas Bram insisted, "The aim of my life is to find the guilty man." Certainly, he knew who was the guilty man. He never insisted he would tell.

POSTSCRIPT

I t remains impossible to know with certainty who killed Charles and Laura Nash and August Blomberg with an axe just before two in the morning of July 14, 1896, on the barkentine *Herbert Fuller* in the middle of the Atlantic Ocean. Of the nine survivors, only three had even a remote opportunity, none of the three had an obvious reason, and only one of the three had a reasonable opportunity. The evidence against the man who went to prison, Thomas Bram, was circumstantial at best. The evidence against the man Bram sought to blame at trial, Charley Brown, was nonexistent. The man who had the greatest opportunity, Lester Monks, was only tangentially accused.

Brown's subsequent life is barely known. Bram's is relatively well known. Monks's lies somewhere in between. If Bram did it, he hid in plain sight for a half century, in prison and out. If Monks did it, at least two people (a family lawyer and a Supreme Court justice) knew or strongly suspected Monks while he was alive, and one person (a prominent Boston lawyer) suggestively implicated Monks seven years after his death.

Mysteries are never solved to the satisfaction of all. That's what makes them mysteries. Whether Lizzie Borden was indeed the axe killer of her father and stepmother—four years before the *Herbert Fuller* murders and fifty miles from the Bram trials—is still fertile ground for speculation, if not about who did it, then how she got away with it. The Borden and *Fuller* murders fit two related genres of fiction, the locked-room mystery and the closed circle of suspects: a house with few home, a ship with few aboard. These murders, though, are fact, which makes their elusive truths ever worth pursuing.

When the *Boston Globe* spoke to Thomas Bram and his *Alvena* crew in January 1929, the paper reflected that the *Herbert Fuller* murders were "one of those unfathomable mysteries destined to discussion . . . until the death of the last person holding it in memory."

If the paper meant every person who had been aboard the ship, the last, Henry Perdok, died in 1952, fifty-six years after the murders. Yet here it is, another seven decades later, and the unfathomable mystery is still under discussion, as close to a conclusion as ever, or no closer at all.

ACKNOWLEDGMENTS

This book began with an endnote. In the appendix to his *Sailing Alone Around the World*, the enduring tale of sea adventure and self-reliance in the dwindling years of the nineteenth century, Joshua Slocum felt compelled by doubters to explain how he had rigged his small sloop to steer itself, a daily necessity over hundreds and thousands of solo ocean miles during his unprecedented journey. In his detailed explanation, Slocum noted briefly that a captain friend of his had testified about the self-steering abilities of ships "in a famous murder trial in Boston, not long since." Slocum was writing in 1900; in 1999, the editor of the Penguin Classics edition of Slocum's book, Thomas Philbrick, provided a substantial endnote, explaining how one Thomas M. Bram had come to be charged, convicted, and "sentenced to life imprisonment at hard labor." I decided I wanted to know more about this Thomas Bram. Now, as one lifelong sailor to two older ones, I thank Joshua Slocum and Thomas Philbrick for pointing me toward Bram, Lester Monks, Charley Brown, the *Herbert Fuller*, and all their troubles.

Essential research was done at the Boston Athenaeum, the Harvard Law School Library, the Massachusetts Historical Society in Boston, and the National Archives in Waltham, Massachusetts, and College Park, Maryland. Special thanks go to Brian Stevens at Western Connecticut State University Archives and Robin Carlaw at the Harvard University Archives. Thanks as well to Elizabeth Bouvier at the Massachusetts Supreme Judicial Court and Cindi Manganello at the Braintree (Massachusetts) Historical Society.

Among many helpful individuals, these stand out: Jim Deibel, Elizabeth Harris, John Higgins, Margaret Horsman, Robert A. G. Monks, Mary Salke, Liz Scull, William Stewart, and Jacqueline Edwards Weir.

At Hachette Books, my thanks to senior production editor Amber Morris, copy editor Annette Wenda, and most of all my longtime editor Bob Pigeon, whose retirement is a challenge to future editors to equal his wisdom and understanding.

As with others before, this book made its way from abstraction to Amazon with the guidance of my agent, Russ Galen, and the patience and advice of my wife, Diane.

NOTES

PROLOGUE

1   *"I am thinking of going"*: This quote appears on page 1230 in the second volume of the three-volume typed and bound transcript of Thomas Bram's first trial. As noted in the Bibliography, the transcripts of the first and second trials can be found in the Harvard Law School Library. Thanks to the efforts of Leslie Schoenfeld, the public services and visual collections administrator for historical and special collections at the library, the transcripts were digitized during my research and can now be found online, with easily searchable text. Any quote that does not have a note will be found readily in the digital transcripts. Thus, to borrow from Richard Nixon, ladies and gentlemen, this is my first and last citation to the trial transcripts.

3   *"rest easy"*: *Boston Globe*, July 21, 1896.

3   *"under the advice"*: Lester Monks (hereafter cited as LM) sworn affidavit, July 23, 1896, US Circuit Court, Massachusetts, Case Papers, #1790, October Term 1896, box 1028, National Archives, Boston (Waltham, Mass.).

1. THE PASSENGER

6   *"He was one"*: "Monks Memorabilia," 44.

6   *"is a potential epic"*: G. Gardner Monks, *Beginnings*, 42.

7   *"a near total"*: Monks, *Beginnings*, 3.

7   *"We were a very"*: "Monks Memorabilia," 90.

8   *"Began poor"*: A. Forbes and G. W. Greene, *The Rich Men of Massachusetts: Containing a Statement of the Reputed Wealth of About Fifteen Hundred Persons, Brief Sketches of More than One Thousand Characters*, 44.

8   *"a very comfortable"*: "Monks Memorabilia," 95.

9   *"hence there was no"*: "Monks Memorabilia," 42.

10   *"was industrious and able"*: "Monks Memorabilia," 142.

10   *"passionately fond of"*: Boston Daily Journal, July 22, 1896.

11   *"There was," wrote one boy*: Henry Jay Case, *Guy Hamilton Scull: Soldier, Writer, Explorer and War Correspondent*, 11–12.

11   *"the youngest helmsman"*: Boston Daily Advertiser, July 23, 1896.

12   *"fast and able"*: Boston Herald, May 28, 1896.

12   *"As an amateur skipper"*: Boston Daily Advertiser, July 23, 1896.

12   *"Lester Monks was trying to see"*: Boston Daily Journal, July 29, 1895.

13   *"on account of sickness"*: LM to Montague Chamberlain, November 8, 1894, in Harvard College Admissions folder for "Monks, Lester Hawthorne s[tudent]1894–96." All the school material items come from this folder.

13   *"bad cold and jams"*: LM, absence form, November 9, 1894.

13   *"His father fears pneumonia"*: M[ontague] C[hamberlain], notation on LM absence form, November 9, 1894.

13   *"is not doing as well"*: Frank Monks to Chamberlain, December 18, 1894.

14   *"a great deal"*: LM to Nathaniel Shaler, January 30, 1896.

14   *"Lester seems now"*: G[eorge] H. Monks to Chamberlain, December 26, 1895.

14   *"having been sick"*: LM to Shaler, January 30, 1896.

14   *"cold and headaches"*: LM, absence form, February 26, 1896.

14   *"in bed with bad knee"*: LM, absence form, May 5, 1896.

14   *"There is not the slightest doubt"*: New York Times, August 12, 1894.

14   *"I have decided"*: LM to Chamberlain, May 25, 1896.

15   *"Doubtless alcohol"*: Monks, *Beginnings*, 42.

15   *"Just before I started"*: Boston Globe, July 23, 1896.

16   *"he still believed in him"*: Ellery Sedgwick, "Adventures by Proxy," 312.

2. THE MATE

18   *"very intelligent and respectable people"*: *Boston Globe*, April 7, 1897.

18   *"of such a genial disposition"*: *Boston Morning Journal*, July 25, 1896.

19   *"Almost from the day"*: *Brooklyn Daily Eagle*, July 22, 1896.

20   *"All our relations"*: George A. Brett, Son & Co., affidavit, February 28, 1890, US Circuit Court, Massachusetts, Case Papers, #1790, October Term 1896, box 1028, National Archives, Boston (Waltham, Mass.).

20   *"When he came to us"*: *Brooklyn Daily Eagle*, July 22, 1896.

21   *"we never had an accident"*: *Boston Globe*, July 23, 1896.

22   *"he came to me and asked me"*: *Brooklyn Daily Eagle*, July 22, 1896.

23   *"I have found him thoroughly competent"*: George Cruse, master, S.S. *Manin*, affidavit, May 5, 1896, US Circuit Court, Massachusetts, Case Papers, #1790, October Term 1896, box 1028, National Archives, Boston (Waltham, Mass.).

23   *"had given complete satisfaction"*: *Boston Globe*, July 23, 1896.

23   *"had a good deal of confidence"*: *Boston Globe*, July 22, 1896.

3. CAST OF OTHER CHARACTERS

27   *"There was not"*: *Boston Globe*, July 22, 1896.

27   *"He held various"*: *Boston Globe*, June 20, 1889.

28   *"It was the same"*: *Philadelphia Times*, January 4, 1893.

28   *"We all lay huddled"*: *New York World*, January 5, 1893.

29   *"The men assert"*: *Delaware Gazette*, June 1, 1893.

29   *"While Capt. Nash"*: *Boston Herald*, July 25, 1896.

29   *"objected to the mate's"*: *Delaware Gazette*, June 1, 1893.

30   *"was very brusk"*: *Boston Herald*, July 30, 1896.

30   *"one of the most"*: *Boston Herald*, July 29, 1896.

32   *"a brunette"*: *Halifax Herald*, July 22, 1896.

32   *"was a splendid woman"*: *Boston Herald*, July 29, 1896.

33   *"What kind of a crew"*: *Boston Globe*, July 23, 1896.

33   *"a small lad"*: *Boston Globe*, February 2, 1897.

35   *"with a view of earning"*: *Boston Globe*, January 1, 1912.

35   *"prominent masseur"*: *Boston Globe*, October 6, 1925.

35   *"had good habits"*: *Boston Globe*, September 5, 1901.

36   *"stubbornly denied"*: *Lowell (MA) Sun*, August 23, 1937.

36   *"Mr. Perdok's love"*: Fitchburg (MA) Sentinel, January 27, 1903.

36   *"without just cause"*: Fitchburg (MA) Sentinel, May 26, 1916.

38   *"pleasant"*: Boston Daily Journal, July 13, 1898.

38   *"was that of"*: Charles E. Grinnell, "Why Thomas Bram Was Found Guilty," 164.

38   *"He was a very quiet"*: Boston Herald, July 25, 1896.

4. LIFE AND DEATH ON BOARD

48   *"Still here with nothing"*: Journal of passenger Lester Hawthorne Monks, a student, 1896 July 1–17, collection relating to the Bram trial, 1895 September 5–1898 April 20, Boston Athanaeum.

50   *"a voluntary cause"*: Boston Globe, July 22, 1896.

51   *"a first rate navigator"*: Boston Globe, July 23, 1896.

56   *"The hands of a part"*: Melville Davisson Post, *The Strange Schemes of Randolph Mason*, 5.

5. TO SHORE

59   *"One of the most"*: Halifax Herald, July 22, 1896.

59   *"For cold blooded"*: Boston Globe, July 22, 1896.

60   *"The stench was frightful"*: Ottawa Journal, July 21, 1896.

60   *"It was a terrible"*: Halifax Herald, July 22, 1896.

60   *"pushed and swayed"*: Ottawa Journal, July 21, 1896.

60   *"Many of them fainted"*: Halifax Herald, July 22, 1896.

60   *"suspected murderer"*: Boston Globe, July 22, 1896.

61   *"Ship at Halifax"*: Boston Globe, July 21, 1896.

61   *"a clever young"*: Winnipeg Daily Free Press, February 29, 1891.

61   *"is the only narrative"*: Washington Evening Times, July 21, 1896.

61   *"Will you write story"*: Goddard to LM telegram, July 22, 1896, copy in author's possession.

63   *"The passenger must have"*: Washington Evening Times, July 21, 1896.

64   *"One of the most mysterious"*: Halifax Herald, July 22, 1896.

64   *"Tuesday, July 14"*: LM statement, collection relating to the Bram trial, 1895 September 5–1898 April 20, Boston Athanaeum.

83   *"On this day"*: Captain's logbook, 1895 September 5–1896 July 17, collection relating to the Bram trial, 1895 September 5–1898 April 20, Boston Athanaeum.

90   *"he became very nervous"*: Boston Herald, July 23, 1896.

90   *"rather disjointed narrative"*: Boston Globe, July 23, 1896.

91   *"He wasn't a drinking"*: Boston Globe, July 22, 1896.

91   *"This reticence"*: Boston Globe, July 23, 1896.

93   *"The strain on young Monck"*: Toronto Globe and Mail, July 23, 1896.

94   *"at sea regarding"*: Boston Globe, July 24, 1896.

94   *"Yes, I have stated"*: Boston Post, July 24, 1896.

95   *"I retired to my cabin"*: LM sworn affidavit, July 23, 1896, US Circuit Court, Massachusetts, Case Papers, #1790, October Term 1896, Box 1028, National Archives, Boston (Waltham, Mass.).

96   *"exonerated from all blame"*: Boston Globe, July 24, 1896.

96   *"Many persons have asked"*: Boston Post, July 24, 1896.

96   *"Somebody ought to erect"*: Boston Herald, July 24, 1896.

97   *"the most colorful"*: Halifax Morning Chronicle, October 3, 1938.

98   *"The police are apparently"*: New York Times, July 24, 1896.

98   *"I assure you"*: Boston Globe, October 17, 1896.

98   *"Although he did not"*: Toronto Globe and Mail, July 24, 1896.

99   *"BROWN A MADMAN?"*: Boston Daily Advertiser, July 25, 1896.

99   *"It is the irony"*: Boston Globe, July 26, 1896.

99   *"neatly dressed"*: Boston Globe, July 27, 1896.

100   *"Good morning"*: Boston Daily Journal, July 28, 1896.

6. TO COURT

102   *"kindness of heart"*: Boston Post, July 29, 1896.

102   *"I ought to get"*: New York Times, July 28, 1896.

102   *"He hardly knew"*: Boston Herald, July 30, 1896.

103   *"one of the ranking"*: New York Times, August 24, 1933.

103   *"Mr. Cotter had a"*: Boston Globe, August 23, 1933.

104   *"The first time we saw"*: Boston Globe, August 3, 1896.

105   *"wrote him encouraging"*: Boston Herald, January 29, 1905.

105   *"It is all something"*: Syracuse Herald, reprinted in Buffalo Morning Express, August 17, 1896.

106   *"manly form"*: Boston Globe, December 10, 1898.

106   *"He has been hunting"*: Boston Daily Journal, October 20, 1896.

107   *"The dead leaves"*: Boston Daily Advertiser, November 2, 1896.

107   *"In the plain language"*: Frederick L. Hoffman, Race Traits and Tendencies of the American Negro, 312, 329.

107   *"In his talk"*: *Boston Herald*, December 24, 1896.

108   *"the identity of the murderer"*: Sedgwick, "Adventures by Proxy," 318.

109   *"My boy, tell me why you did it."*: Sedgwick, "Adventures by Proxy," 318

109   *"It will be"*: *Boston Herald*, December 14, 1896.

111   *"To me killing isn't"*: Ryūnosuke Akutagawa, "In a Grove," in *Rashomon, and Other Stories*, 27.

122   *"My conscience says"*: *Boston Globe*, December 21, 1896.

125   *"The Verdict a Surprise"*: *Boston Sunday Herald*, January 3, 1897.

125   *"May God forgive me"*: *Albany Law Journal*, January 9, 1897.

125   *"I voted for"*: *Boston Post*, January 4, 1897.

125   *"We had good debaters"*: *Boston Sunday Herald*, January 3, 1897.

126   *"voted against our convictions"*: *Boston Post*, January 4, 1897.

126   *"I am an innocent"*: *Boston Sunday Herald*, January 3, 1897.

126   *"fair and conservative course"*: *Boston Morning Journal*, January 4, 1897.

127   *"it is generally conceded"*: *Albany Law Journal*, January 16, 1897.

127   *"He sleeps well"*: *Boston Post*, February 23, 1897.

128   *"In the presence of"*: *New York Times*, March 10, 1897.

129   *"The rule is not"*: *Bram v. United States*, 168 U.S. 532, at 549.

129   *"mind the fear that"*: *Bram v. United States*, 168 U.S. 532, at 562.

129   *"Bram had been brought"*: *Bram v. United States*, 168 U.S. 532, at 563.

129   *"in order to be admissible"*: *Bram v. United States*, 168 U.S. 532, at 542–543.

130   *"I am glad"*: *Boston Globe*, December 14, 1897.

131   *"shall be sentenced to"*: United States, 54th Congress, Session 2, Chapter 29, January 15, 1897.

131   *"More than 1000 people"*: *Boston Globe*, March 19, 1898.

134   *"Monks, honest boy"*: *Boston Globe*, April 20, 1898.

135   *"exceedingly brief"*: *Boston Globe*, April 21, 1898.

135   *"Guilty, but without"*: *Boston Evening Transcript*, April 21, 1898.

135   *"surprised by the verdict"*: *Boston Evening Transcript*, April 21, 1898.

135   *"as though mentally"*: *Boston Globe*, April 21, 1898.

136   *"I can only refresh"*: *Boston Daily Advertiser*, July 13, 1898.

7. A MOST UNFORTUNATE ENDING

137   *"The bullet entered"*: *Boston Globe*, April 19, 1900.

138 *"the most beautiful"*: *New York World*, May 11, 1900.

139 *"extremely pretty and"*: *Washington Post*, April 21, 1900.

139 *"in which Boston feels"*: *Boston Home Journal*, April 21, 1900.

139 *"Brilliant Wedding"*: *New York World*, May 11, 1900.

140 *"to be congratulated"*: *Black Diamond*, February 20, 1904, 444.

140 *"one of the most important"*: *Boston Sunday Post*, July 2, 1904.

140 *"The deal is of"*: *Black Diamond*, July 30, 1904, 287.

140 *"a prominent coal man"*: *Black Diamond*, December 3, 1904, 1223.

140 *"for the purpose of"*: *Black Diamond*, December 31, 1904, 1428.

141 *"a surly fellow"*: *Boston Morning Journal*, March 29, 1903.

141 *"extensively entertained"*: *Boston Sunday Globe*, April 7, 1901.

141 *"temporarily deserted her"*: *Boston Post*, April 3, 1904.

141 *"beautiful specimen"*: *Daily Kennebec Journal*, May 20, 1904.

141 *"a very charming"*: *Boston Post*, October 26, 1902.

142 *"adequate service"*: *Boston Post*, October 16, 1909.

142 *"a long and continuous"*: Copy of Libel and Order, *Frances F. L. Monks v. Lester H. Monks*, Norfolk County (MA) Superior Court, February 28, 1911.

143 *"Divorce Defendant Prominent"*: *Boston Post*, September 2, 1911.

143 *"quite a succession"*: *Boston Sunday Post*, December 17, 1911.

144 *"patience finally came"*: Monks, *Beginnings*, 45.

144 *"landed in Seattle"*: "Letters of a Down-and-Out," *Atlantic Monthly*, February 1913.

147 *"It's getting pretty gray"*: "Letters of a Down-and-Out," *Atlantic Monthly*, March 1913.

151 *"long known"*: Sedgwick, "Adventures by Proxy," 312.

151 *"scion of one of Boston's"*: *Selma (AL) Times-Journal*, September 30, 1913; it seems likely that the Alabama paper was reprinting a wire-service or Boston newspaper story that eluded me.

151 *"It must have been"*: Sedgwick, "Adventures by Proxy," 310.

152 *"From earliest boyhood"*: Sedgwick, "Adventures by Proxy," 311.

152 *"in a bath of blood"*: Sedgwick, "Adventures by Proxy," 314.

152 *"did more to strengthen"*: Sedgwick to Rev. John C. Petrie, October 1, 1946, Sedgwick Papers, Massachusetts Historical Society.

153 *"From 1910 to 1915"*: *Twenty-Fifth Anniversary Report*, Harvard College Class of 1898 (1923), 378.

153 *"very quietly"*: *Washington Post*, September 7, 1913.

154 *"whose family has been"*: A Souvenir of New York City, Old and New (1918), 300.

154 *"It was only the work"*: *Atlanta Constitution*, December 29, 1945.

8. BRAM UNBOUND

157 *"a man sentenced"*: *Boston Herald*, July 22, 1906.

158 *"a true and loyal"*: *Boston Herald*, November 25, 1906.

158 *"I have reached"*: Daniel W. Rountree to James A. Finch, February 16, 1911, in Bram Pardon File.

158 *"convinced all of"*: Rountree to Finch, March 11, 1911, in Bram Pardon File.

159 *"all of his actions"*: William H. Moyer to Finch, March 16, 1911, in Bram Pardon File.

159 *"a model prisoner"*: H. A. MacDonald to French, March 17, 1911, in Bram Pardon File.

159 *"His cheerfulness is"*: [____] Fry to French, March 17, 1911, in Bram Pardon File.

159 *"Bram is as tender"*: A. L. Fowler to French, March 17, 1911, in Bram Pardon File.

159 *"as a prisoner and a man"*: T. C. Tupper to Finch, March 18, 1911, in Bram Pardon File.

160 *"I think well of him"*: Everett C. Herrick to Finch, December 24, 1911, in Bram Pardon File.

160 *"He has always been"*: Jonathan W. Boyle to French, March 17, 1911, in Bram Pardon File.

160 *"absolutely innocent"*: Thomas Bram pardon application, March 11, 1911, in Bram Pardon File.

161 *"We have both always"*: French to Finch, December 4, 1911, in Bram Pardon File.

161 *"[T]he pardon of this man"*: Boyd Jones to George Wickersham, December 19, 1911, in Bram Pardon File.

161 *"I have not entertained"*: Boyd Jones to Finch, February 21, 1912, in Bram Pardon File.

161 *"I cannot conscientiously"*: LeBaron Colt to French, February 13, 1912, in Bram Pardon File.

161 *"a man of strong likes"*: William H. Dunbar, "Ezra Ripley Thayer," 8.

161   *"if there could be"*: Ezra Ripley Thayer to Winfred T. Denison, December 21, 1911, in Bram Pardon File.

162   *"while in a state of"*: *New York Times*, September 17, 1915.

162   *"Now what I want"*: H. L. Bram to Mr. President [Taft], February 26, 1912, in Bram Pardon File.

162   *"I am opposed to"*: *Boston Globe*, January 1, 1912.

162   *"confidently expected"*: *Detroit Free Press*, February 12, 1912.

163   *"a poor, penniless"*: Bram to Wickersham, August 28, 1912, in Bram Pardon File.

163   *"I have studied"*: *Boston Globe*, September 19, 1912.

163   *"wholly blameless"*: Julian Hawthorne, *The Subterranean Brotherhood*, 145.

163   *"Mr. Moyer is the"*: *Atlanta Constitution*, October 17, 1913.

164   *"Brown accused me"*: *Boston Globe*, August 28, 1913.

164   *"I do hope"*: Bram to Moyer August 28, 1913, in National Archives, https://research.archives.gov/id/646360.

165   *"I am greatly pleased"*: *Boston Post*, August 29, 1913.

165   *"Few convicts have ever"*: *Boston Sunday Herald*, September 14, 1913.

165   *"engaged by the family"*: Gordon Ireland, *The Balestiers of Beechwood*, 23.

166   *"Bram is out"*: *Boston Post*, August 29, 1913.

166   *"It was the Summer"*: *Boston Globe*, March 22, 1914.

167   *"to say to you"*: Bram to Roger Scaife, January 19, 1914, in Mary Roberts Rinehart Papers, Archives & Special Collections, University of Pittsburgh Library, https://digital.library.pitt.edu/islandora/object/pitt%3A31735037972043.

168   *"Mr. Bram, I am"*: *Atlanta Constitution*, September 4, 1913.

168   *"A start"*: *Atlanta Constitution*, September 28, 1913.

168   *"One of the best"*: J. W. Whitaker to Thomas W. Gregory, October 7, 1915, Bram Pardon File.

169   *"He was convicted by"*: *Atlantian*, November 1914.

169   *"The evidence which fastened"*: Bram to the President of the United States, October 11, 1915, Bram Pardon File.

169   *"five years' probation"*: Pardon Attorney to F. H. Duehay, February 2, 1916, Bram Pardon File.

169   *"I left the Railroad"*: Bram to Finch, August 28, 1918, Bram Pardon File.

170   *"I see no special":* Thomas Watt Gregory to Finch, March 15, 1916, Bram Pardon File.

170   *"I was present at":* Memorandum for the Attorney General by Mr. Warren, November 15, 1916, Bram Pardon File.

171   *"Many of my personal":* Thomas Hardwick to Attorney General, January 27, 1917, Bram Pardon File.

9. REDEMPTION

174   *"a neutral vessel":* Miami Herald, February 21, 1917.

175   *"Ill Luck Follows":* Brooklyn Daily Eagle, July 17, 1898.

176   *"down by the head":* Brooklyn Daily Eagle, March 1, 1900.

176   *"serious injuries":* Brooklyn Daily Eagle, December 31, 1900.

176   *"He has been drinking":* New York Times, June 24, 1897.

176   *"to put any more":* Herbert Fuller to Swan & Son, June 27, 1910, in Gloria de Prado, "The Herbert Fuller and New York's Shipping Industry from 1890–1910," 130.

177   *"one of the most":* Brooklyn Daily Eagle, June 15, 1916.

177   *"Negro mate":* Boston Herald, May 30, 1917.

177   *"Information Cheerfully Furnished":* Annalist, various issues, March–June 1918.

178   *"one of the largest ever":* Eastern Underwriter, June 11, 1920.

179   *"to prove my worthiness":* Bram to Finch, December 6, 1917, in Bram Pardon File.

180   *"It should not be":* A. Mitchell Palmer to President Wilson, April 7, 1919, in Bram Pardon File.

180   *"full and unconditional":* Boston Globe, June 19, 1919.

180   *"lapse of time always":* Memorandum for the Attorney General, April 2, 1919, Bram Pardon File.

181   *"pardon again brings":* Boston Globe, June 19, 1919.

10. JOYS AND SORROWS

183   *"Edward, you will want":* Sedgwick, "Adventures by Proxy," 320.

184   *"undying gratitude":* Bram to French, July 30, 1921, in Sermons Collected by Thomas Bram, Harvard Law School Library.

185   *"the new shipping king":* Boston Post, July 20, 1920.

185 *"to devote all his time"*: New-York Tribune, October 18, 1920.

185 *"amicable, that he will"*: New York Times, October 14, 1920.

185 *"For quite a while"*: Monks, *Beginnings*, 48.

186 *"I looked over"*: Clarence W. Barron, *They Told Barron: Conversations and Revelations of an American Pepys in Wall Street*, 72.

186 *"When he left the house"*: Monks, *Beginnings*, 49.

187 *"When Justice Triumphed"*: New York Daily News, February 6, 1927.

187 *"her constant hope"*: Monks, *Beginnings*, 49.

187 *"L. H. Monks' Death"*: Boston Globe, September 13, 1927.

188 *"His was a life"*: Monks, *Beginnings*, 49.

189 *"associated with use of alcohol"*: Registry Division of the City of Boston, Death Certificate No. 540950, Lester H. Monks, May 2, 2017.

189 *"I trust and hope"*: Twenty-fifth Anniversary Report, Harvard College Class of 1898 (1923), 378.

189 *"Drinking habits recurred"*: Monks, *Beginnings*, 36.

190 *"A good wife is to be"*: Princeton University *Alumni Weekly*, April 4, 2012.

190 *"I am innocent"*: Boston Post, January 3, 1897.

190 *"Slayer of Three"*: New York Sun, January 11, 1928.

191 *"for a crime said to"*: Atlanta Constitution, January 11, 1928.

191 *"loss of Mate Bram"*: New York Sun, January 12, 1928.

191 *"there has been silence"*: Baltimore Sun, January 11, 1928.

191 *"as a precautionary measure"*: New York Times, January 14, 1928.

191 *"after a sailor in Los Angeles"*: Atlanta Constitution, January 14, 1928.

191 *"The land holds little"*: Boston Globe, January 28, 1929.

192 *"long regarded as"*: New York Times, August 24, 1933.

192 *"Sea Mystery Recalled"*: Hartford Courant, August 24, 1933.

193 *"a long courtship"*: Boston Globe September 6, 1930.

193 *"to warrant her living"*: Boston Globe, September 26, 1933.

193 *"his advanced age"*: Boston Globe, September 18, 1935.

194 *"On his death-bed"*: Richard Hale to Eldon James, December 21, 1933, tipped into *United States v. Bram* (1896), vol. 1, typed transcript, Harvard Law School Library.

194 *"I was intimate with"*: Alfred Worcester to Eldon James, March 27, 1939, tipped into *United States v. Thomas Bram* (1896), vol. 1, typed transcript, Harvard Law School Library.

195 *"dine and dance"*: San Francisco Examiner, June 28, 1939.
196 *"retired real estate broker"*: Miami News, March 31, 1947.

POSTSCRIPT

198 *"one of those unfathomable"*: Boston Globe, January 28, 1929.

BIBLIOGRAPHY

MANUSCRIPTS AND LEGAL MATERIAL

"The After House" (1914). Box 19, folder 2, Mary Roberts Rinehart Papers, 1831–1970. Special Collections Department, University of Pittsburgh. https://digital.library.pitt.edu/islandora/object/pitt%3A 31735037972043.

Bram, Thomas. Case file, Pardon Case Files, 1853–1946. Office of the Pardon Attorney, Department of Justice, National Archives, College Park, MD.

Bram v. United States, 168 U.S. 532, Case No. 340, U.S. Supreme Court, 1897.

Collection Relating to the Bram trial. Boston Athenaeum.

Harvard College Admissions folder for Lester Hawthorne Monks. Harvard University Archives.

"Monks Memorabilia," a compendium of family-related written materials, compiled circa 1894–2002. Privately held.

Sedgwick, Ellery. Papers. Massachusetts Historical Society, Boston.

Sermons Collected by Thomas M. C. Bram while in the Massachusetts State Prison at Charlestown (1898–1907) under sentence of life imprisonment for the murder on the high seas, July 14, 1896, of Charles I. Nash, Master of the Barkentine, the *Herbert Fuller*, and of his wife, Laura A. Nash, 1898–1921. Manuscript. Historical and Special Collections, Harvard Law School Library.

United States v. Thomas Bram. Circuit Court of the United States, 1896. 4 vols., typewritten (carbon copy). Harvard Law School Library. https://listview.lib.harvard.edu/lists/drs-433888700.

United States v. Thomas Bram. Circuit Court of the United States, 1898. 4 vols., typewritten (carbon copy). Harvard Law School Library. https://listview.lib.harvard.edu/lists/drs-433888722.

US Circuit Court, Massachusetts. Case Papers, #1790, October Term 1896, box 1028. National Archives, Boston (Waltham, Mass.)

PERIODICALS

Albany Law Journal
Annalist: A Magazine of Finance, Commerce and Economics
Atlanta Constitution
Boston Daily Advertiser
Boston Daily Journal
Boston Globe
Boston Herald
Boston Morning Journal
Brooklyn Daily Eagle
Eastern Underwriter
Halifax Herald
New York Times
New-York Tribune
Ottawa Journal

OTHER SOURCES

Akutagawa, Ryūnosuke. "In a Grove." Translated by Takashi Kojima. In *Rashomon, and Other Stories.* New York: Liveright, 1952.

Barron, Clarence W. *They Told Barron: Conversations and Revelations of an American Pepys in Wall Street.* New York: Harper & Bros., 1930.

Beer, Thomas. *The Mauve Decade: American Life at the End of the Nineteenth Century.* 1926. Reprint, New York: Carroll & Graf, 1997.

Brennan-Marquez, Kiel, and Stephen E. Henderson. "Fourth Amendment Anxiety." *American Criminal Law Review* 5, no. 1 (2018): 1–35.

Brooks, Van Wyck. *The Confident Years: 1885–1915.* New York: Dutton, 1952.

Caldwell, Laura, and Leslie S. Klinger, eds. *Anatomy of Innocence: Testimonies of the Wrongfully Convicted.* New York: Liveright, 2017.

Case, Henry Jay. *Guy Hamilton Scull: Soldier, Writer, Explorer and War Correspondent*. New York: Duffield, 1922.

Cohen, Daniel. *The Encyclopedia of Unsolved Crimes*. New York: Dorset Press, 1988.

de Prado, Gloria. "The Herbert Fuller and New York's Shipping Industry from 1890–1910." Master's thesis, Western Connecticut State University, 1994.

Dunbar, William H. "Ezra Ripley Thayer." *Harvard Law Review* 29, no. 1 (1915).

Forbes, A., and J. W. Greene. *The Rich Men of Massachusetts: Containing a Statement of the Reputed Wealth of About Fifteen Hundred Persons, Brief Sketches of More than One Thousand Characters*. Boston: W. V. Spencer, 1851.

Grinnell, Charles E. "Why Thomas Bram Was Found Guilty." *Green Bag* 9, no. 4 (1897): 146–168.

Grisham, John. *The Innocent Man*. New York: Doubleday, 2006.

Hanson, Neil. *The Custom of the Sea*. New York: John Wiley & Sons, 1999.

Hawthorne, Julian. *The Subterranean Brotherhood*. New York: McBride, Nast, 1914.

Hiam, C. Michael. *Murder Aboard: The* Herbert Fuller *Tragedy and the Ordeal of Thomas Bram*. Guilford, CT: Lyons Press, 2019.

Hoffman, Frederick L. *Race Traits and Tendencies of the American Negro*. New York: Macmillan, 1896.

Hopkin, Alannah, and Kathy Bunney. *The Ship of Seven Murders: A True Story of Madness and Murder*. Cork, Ireland: Collins Press, 2010.

Ireland, Gordon. "The Balestiers of Beechwood." Typescript. Washington, DC, 1948.

Langewiesche, William. *The Outlaw Sea: A World of Freedom, Chaos, and Crime*. New York: North Point Press, 2004.

Logan, Guy. "Mystery of the *Herbert Fuller*." In *Wilful Murder: Studies of Notable Crimes*, 166–189. London: Eldon Press, 1935.

Minot, George E. "The Mystery of the Barkentine *Fuller*." In *Murder Will Out*, 13–25. Boston: Marshall Jones, 1928.

Monks, G. Gardner. *Beginnings*. Portland, ME: Colonial Printing, 1978.

Nash, Jay Robert. *Murder, America: Homicide in the United States from the Revolution to the Present*. New York: Simon and Schuster, 1980.

Pearson, Edmund. "Mate Bram!" In *Studies in Murder*, 169–240. New York: Random House, 1938.

Philbrick, Nathaniel. *In the Heart of the Sea: The Tragedy of the Whaleship Essex*. New York: Penguin, 2000.

Post, Melville Davisson. *The Strange Schemes of Randolph Mason*. New York: G. P. Putnam's Sons, 1896.

Raddall, Thomas H. "The Murders Aboard the *Herbert Fuller*." In *Footsteps on Old Floors*, 43–94. Garden City, NY: Doubleday, 1986.

Rinehart, Mary Roberts. *The After House*. Boston: Houghton Mifflin, 1914.

Saltzburg, Stephen. "*Miranda v. Arizona* Revisited: Constitutional Law or Judicial Fiat." *Washburn Law Journal* 26, no. 1 (1986): 1–26.

Schecter, Harold. *Hell's Princess: The Mystery of Belle Gunness, Butcher of Men*. New York: Little A, 2018.

Sedgwick, Ellery. "Adventures by Proxy." In *The Happy Profession*, 306–320. Boston: Little, Brown, 1946.

Stevenson, Robert Louis. *The Wrecker*. New York: Charles Scribner's Sons, 1903.

Warden, Rob, and Steven A. Drizin. "Thomas M. Bram." In *True Stories of False Confessions*, 283–287. Evanston, IL: Northwestern University Press, 2009.

INDEX